KU-724-149

BEYOND DECORATION

Beyond Decoration

The illustrations of John Everett Millais

PAUL GOLDMAN

THE BRITISH LIBRARY
PRIVATE LIBRARIES ASSOCIATION
OAK KNOLL PRESS

Published by The British Library.
96 Euston Road, London NW1 2DB, England

Private Libraries Association,
Ravelston, South View Road, Pinner,
Middlesex HA5 3YD, England

Oak Knoll Press
310 Delaware Sreet, New Castle,
Delaware 19720, U.S.A.

ISBN
0 7123 4775 5 (The British Library)
1 900002 57 3 (Private Libraries Association)
1 58456 135 1 (Oak Knoll Press)

A CIP Catalogue record for this book is
available from the British Library

Library of Congress Cataloging-in-Publication Data
Goldman, Paul.
Beyond decoration: the illustrations of
John Everett Millais / Paul Goldman.
p. cm
Includes bibliographical references and index.
ISBN 1 58456 135 1 (Oak Knoll)
ISBN 0 7123 4775 5 (British Library)
ISBN 1 900002 57 3 (Private Libraries Association)
1. Millais, John Everett, Sir, 1829–1896 –
criticism and interpretation.
2. Illustration of books – Great Britain – 19th century.
3. Illustration of books, Victorian – Great Britain.
4. Pre-Raphaelitism – Great Britain.
I. Millais, John Everett, Sir, 1829–1896. II. Title.
NC978.5.M55G65 2004
741.6'4'092–dc22 2004056079

Designed and typeset by
David Chambers

Printed in Great Britain by the
St Edmundsbury Press

for
Corinna
as always, and
in memory of my mother,
June

CONTENTS

Acknowledgements

As with any project of this kind there are numerous people to thank for help, guidance and encouragement. I particularly wish to express my gratitude to the following: John Allitt, Geoffrey Beare, the late W.E. (Dick) Fredeman, Colin Harrison, Valerie Holman, Simon Houfe, Clive Hurst, Elizabeth James, Edmund King, Rupert Maas, Julia Nurse, Maroussia Oakley, Frances Rankine, Leonard Roberts, Daniel Slive, Angela and John Thirlwell, Christine Wise and Malcolm Warner. Special debts are owed to Robin de Beaumont, who has been my constant mentor and adviser in the field for so many years, and Geoffroy Millais, who has also offered unfailing kindly assistance from an unique family standpoint. Both have read the text in draft and made enormously valuable suggestions which I have been grateful to incorporate. David Way at British Library Publishing has been my chief supporter in bringing this difficult proposal to a handsome conclusion and further thanks are due to Kathleen Houghton and Catherine Britton, also at the press, who have been always helpful and willing throughout. I must thank David Chambers for providing a most sympathetic design. His attention to detail and commitment to the project have proved invaluable. Finally, my gratitude goes to Johanna Stephenson for being a forbearing and meticulous copy-editor.

The majority of the illustrations have been scanned by David Chambers from copies in my own collection; others have been taken from copies in The British Library, the British Museum, the University of London Library, and the Victoria and Albert Museum. In addition, I must acknowledge the staff of the following institutions who have helped in innumerable ways in providing research facilities: The British Museum, Department of Prints and Drawings; The British Library, Department of Printed Books and Music Library; The University of London (Senate House) Library; The Victoria and Albert Museum (National Art Library); The Museum of Fine Arts, Boston; The National Gallery of Australia, Canberra; The Library of Congress, Washington; and the Ashmolean Museum, Oxford.

My greatest debt, however, is to my wife, Corinna, who has not only borne the presence of Millais as an illustrator in our house over several years but has also listened with patience to repeated readings of the text and proved a stern but just critic.

Paul Goldman

Introduction

This book is intended to provide a new approach to the book and periodical illustrations of Millais. The title 'Beyond Decoration' is chosen not just for mellifluousness, but to signify my belief that the contribution he made to this branch of art elevated its status to a higher intellectual level than it had been accorded hitherto. While not primarily a bibliographical study, certain significant details are provided in the two sections devoted to listings. More detailed references will be found in a previous study.[1] However, provided here are the literary contexts for each design, and it is the relationship between the image and the text which forms the central theme of the present work. Hence my assertion that the current essay is somewhat novel and reasonably comprehensive, notwithstanding the existence of two noteworthy predecessors.[2] While the emphasis on Millais and Trollope is understandable on account of the undeniable interest and quality of the work, it is by no means the entire story. My aim, while duly acknowledging what has been previously written, is to try to reveal both a more profound and a wider-ranging artist than perhaps has been earlier perceived.

Millais was not just the most prolific of the Pre-Raphaelite illustrators but he was also the more varied, both in his themes and in his styles. For example, he could draw with equal facility for children or for adults and was as much at home with the historical novel as with those of Trollope, which were set in the contemporary world.[3] However, in one further respect I believe I see an additional aspect to the interest in Millais's work as an illustrator. By isolating and identifying the particular 'moment' in a poem or story which the artist chooses to illustrate, I trust it may be possible to understand, in a more complete way, what he is doing or attempting to achieve.

The debt Millais owed to his engravers was immense and he worked closely with them, especially the Dalziel Brothers. Another entire book would be required to examine in detail the extent of their involvement and the process and industrial practice of nineteenth century wood-engraving. Some relevant issues have been dealt with in my two previous studies (see Select Bibliography) but for more information I refer the reader to the work of Rodney Engen.[4]

The scheme in the listings in this volume is as follows. For the books, which are organised chronologically, the order is: author, title, publisher, British Library or other collection reference, description of design including

1 *Victorian Illustration: The Pre-Raphaelites, The Idyllic School and the High Victorians*, London: Lund Humphries, 2004.
2 Mason 1978, pp.309–40; Hall 1980.
3 For examples of the former see [Jean Ingelow], *Studies for Stories from Girls' Lives*, 1866. For the latter see the designs in *Once a Week* for the tales of Harriet Martineau.
4 See especially Rodney Engen, *Dictionary of Victorian Wood Engravers*, Cambridge: Chadwyck-Healey, 1985, which also contains an extensive bibliography.

medium and engraver, measurements (height before width), position in text and literary context. For the periodicals (which appear in alphabetical order), the designs are listed chronologically within each periodical, with the title of the design (where identified), date, position in text, engraver, measurements and author (and on occasion title of work).

Editions referred to are the first that contain relevant illustrations. Square brackets around dates denote that the item is undated but the date is known from an external source. British Library and other press-marks and location references are similarly enclosed in square brackets. BM denotes British Museum, Department of Prints and Drawings. In the listings, the two bookplates designed by Millais are omitted.[5] Initial letter vignette designs are mentioned but not measured. In certain instances, notably for the periodical *Good Words*, it has not always proved possible to give the month of publication of a particular design. This is because dates only appeared on the wrappers of the periodical and these were almost invariably discarded when it was bound up. Sadly, copies in libraries only rarely retain these fascinating and informative sheets of paper. Millais's small oeuvre in etching is listed with the book illustrations, but I make no attempt to catalogue the different states. Similarly I omit details of the prints made after Millais's paintings, chiefly because I do not regard then as being part of his illustrated work; Rodney Engen in his *Pre-Raphaelite Prints* (1995) lists over sixty examples. Works referred to in the footnotes by author's name only are listed in the bibliography, pp. 65-6.

Exact page references in the periodicals are given where the design is untitled, and where I have been able to ascertain, often with difficulty, just which event is being illustrated. The illustrations themselves are regularly placed nowhere near the relevant text and, in certain instances, I have erred on the side of caution and perhaps with cowardice opted to remain uncertain. Sometimes, in the case perhaps of a frontispiece, no context is evident or clear and there are also occasions where it seems the artist has made a drawing suggested by the text rather than one directly influenced by it. In all such cases this uncertainty is shamelessly admitted. By discussing the relationship of image to text, and with the designs to hand, I hope it will prove possible to perceive more clearly the sense and meaning of the illustrations. It is a mistake to see them divorced from their settings, for, without the relevant poem or novel alongside, an entire element is obscured or even lost. It is essential to attempt to identify and analyse exactly what Millais does with a text and the special manner of his accomplishment.

5 For details of Millais's bookplates see Suriano 2000, pp.161ff.

CHAPTER ONE

Millais and the Art of Illustration

IN 1855 GEORGE ROUTLEDGE PUBLISHED A small book of poems by William Allingham entitled *The Music Master, A Love Song, and Two Series of Day and Night Songs*. This apparently unremarkable event was to prove of immense interest and influence in the story and development of British book illustration, for this tiny volume contained wood-engravings by three leading artists of a Pre-Raphaelite nature – Dante Gabriel Rossetti, Arthur Hughes and Millais. While the designs by Hughes are relatively slight and even unconfident, the 'Maids of Elfen-mere' by Rossetti was to prove probably the most influential on the other Pre-Raphaelites. Burne-Jones, writing anonymously the following year reacted to it with passion:

> ... it is I think the most beautiful drawing for an illustration I have ever seen, the weird faces of the maids of Elfinmere [*sic*], the musical timed movement of their arms together as they sing, the face of the man, above all, are such as only a great artist could conceive.[1]

It is from this design that an entirely new approach to book illustration was soon to emerge. Rossetti's drawing is both mysterious yet also disquietingly realistic, and it contains several quintessential Pre-Raphaelite features. The lines are sharply delineated and the figures are not cyphers but redolent of feeling and powerful emotion. The design has a border and is richly and darkly printed. The figure of the man, which so impressed Burne-Jones, is contorted and viewed boldly from behind. Perhaps more than any other feature is the feeling that the image is presented on an equal footing with the text. The artist brings a potent intellect to bear on the task of illustration.

The background from which this image sprang so suddenly was a very contrasting one. The books of the 1830s and 1840s were illustrated by numerous distinguished artists, yet the appearance of their designs was utterly different. The style of George Cruikshank, Robert Seymour and Hablot Knight Browne (Phiz), to name but three, for the works of authors such as Dickens, Charles Lever and William Harrison Ainsworth is essentially, to my mind, more subservient and deferential to the text. For example, the influence of the single-sheet satires of the period 1790–1830 is frequently apparent with an emphasis on wiry lines, stereotyped facial

1 Unsigned essay on 'The Newcomes', *Oxford and Cambridge Magazine*, no.6, 1856.

expressions and somewhat static and conventional poses and stances. This style may perhaps, with caution, be termed 'Theatrical' and examples are numerous. In 'Mrs. Bardell faints in Mr. Pickwick's Arms' by Browne, for which the artist made two versions, several of these elements are to the fore. First is a delicate and delightfully airy etched line; second is a somewhat generalised handling of emotion. There is fear, consternation, concern and anger to be sure, but the atmosphere is regularly one of exaggeration and even caricature. Similarly the poses are conventional and studied: the feeling has much to do with the stage, where movements of hands, legs and bodies must be clear to allow the spectator direct access to the action and to the mood. In the second version the details of the room are more strongly defined by Browne. The clock, picture and bookshelves have been rendered with telling detail.[2] Yet there are still further points of difference. Many of these designs appear as vignettes and the printing, with notable exceptions, is frequently light.[3] It was against a background of much admirable work by the artists just mentioned and many others, including William Mulready and Daniel Maclise, that the Pre-Raphaelites appeared as illustrators.[4]

The grandeur of 'The Maids of Elfen-mere' and its undoubted influence have, to some extent, inevitably overshadowed Millais's single drawing for the same book.

70 This was 'The Fireside Story' which accompanied a poem entitled 'Frost
in the Holidays' and, in its own way, is as remarkable as Rossetti's more
celebrated design.[5] Here also is a powerful composition, strongly delineated
and with a similarly absorbing atmosphere of emotion and deep feeling. Yet,
despite the importance of these two images being printed in the same
outstanding volume, Millais's first published illustration had already
69 appeared some three years earlier.[6] This is an etched frontispiece vignette,
perhaps with more than a glance back at Browne and Cruikshank, but here
in contrast many genuine Pre-Raphaelite characteristics are already noticeable. There is the sharply defined realism, the sense of emotional interaction and also a typically Millaisian feature: a mastery and understanding of contemporary dress. The stylistic changes wrought by Millais and the other Pre-Raphaelite illustrators had begun to emerge even at this early date.

How then does Millais really differ from Rossetti, Holman Hunt, Ford Madox Brown and Burne-Jones, the leading artists who were at the centre of Pre-Raphaelitism? First, he was far more prolific than they were in produc-

2 Charles Dickens, *The Posthumous Papers of the Pickwick Club*, 1836–7, issued in monthly parts, illustrated by Robert Seymour, R.W. Buss and Hablot Knight Browne. For a masterly discussion of this period of illustration see John Harvey, *Victorian Novelists and their Illustrators*, London: Sidgwick and Jackson, 1970.

3 There are several notable exceptions to this assertion. For example in *Bleak House*, issued in monthly parts during 1852–3 and illustrated by H. K. Browne, there appear several of Browne's so-called 'dark' plates. One of the finest is 'The Morning' and it is very different in feeling, mood and emphasis from the large majority of this artist's illustrations.

4 See Oliver Goldsmith, *The Vicar of Wakefield*, London: John Van Voorst, 1843, illustrated by Mulready, and Thomas Moore, *Irish Melodies*, London: Longman, Brown, Green and Longman, 1846, illustrated by Maclise, for arguably these artists' masterpieces in book-illustration.

5 Book Illustrations 3 (1855).

6 W. Wilkie Collins, *Mr. Wray's Cash-Box*, London: Richard Bentley, 1852 (Book Illustrations 2).

ing over three hundred designs for books and periodicals. Secondly, he made illustrations over a longer period – from 1850 until the mid-1880s, although it must be admitted that some of the late designs are likely to have been first drawn at an earlier period.[7] Rossetti and the others made far fewer illustrations than Millais and they also abandoned the task considerably earlier.[8] Nevertheless, it should be stressed also that Millais can only be considered a prolific illustrator when compared to the other Pre-Raphaelites: from the period before him, both Browne and George Cruikshank produced more designs, and in later years artists such as William Heath Robinson and Gordon Browne made a greater quantity of drawings both for books and for periodicals. There are, however, still further features that mark out Millais from his Pre-Raphaelite fellows. While they were chiefly restricted, by and large, to poetry, usually of a Tennysonian kind, both temperamentally and stylistically, so Millais drew for a larger variety of literature and in a number of styles.[9]

The categories of literature for which he drew include adult poetry, with examples such as 'The Moxon Tennyson' and other anthologies.[10] He made many designs for adult prose, notably for several of the novels of Trollope and for the so-called 'Historiettes' of Harriet Martineau.[11] He also produced drawings for children's books, and for works intended specifically for girls.[12] In addition there are the religious texts which prompted him to produce arguably some of his greatest illustrations: *The Parables of Our Lord*. Twelve images were published in *Good Words* of 1863 and all twenty were published in book form and printed on better paper the following year.

Some other subdivisions of activity might be usefully defined, for example the unjustly neglected steel-engraved frontispieces he made for Hurst and Blackett's *Standard Library* Series, and the series of drawings for poems translated from the Breton by Tom Taylor.[13]

However, it is also important to stress once again the fact pinpointed acutely by a previous critic that Millais's relationship with Trollope was 'the only instance where the resources of this rich activity in illustration were put at the service of an important working novelist in a sustained way.'[14] This is

7 See especially Book Illustrations 63 in this connection.

8 Rossetti, for example, made just ten designs for four books between 1855 and 1866, while Burne-Jones produced only eight during the period of the 1860s. I do not include for this purpose, the latter's drawings made for William Morris in the 1890s.

9 There are, however, some interesting exceptions. For Burne-Jones see the extraordinary and uncharacteristic designs he made for [Archibald Maclaren], *The Fairy Family*, London: Longman and Co., 1857. Holman Hunt made a moving drawing in a book for children, 'A Morning Song of Praise', in Isaac Watts, *Divine and Moral Songs for Children*, London: James Nisbet and Co., 1867.

10 See Book Illustrations 6 (1857). Another important anthology of this kind is R.A. Willmott (ed.), *The Poets of the Nineteenth Century* (Book Illustrations 7).

11 The details of the latter will be found under the entries for *Once a Week* (Periodical Illustrations 9).

12 See Book Illustrations 32: Henry Leslie, *Little Songs for Me to Sing* (1865) and no. 19: Sarah Tytler, *Papers for Thoughtful Girls* (1863).

13 For an example of the former see Book Illustrations 13: Dinah Mulock (Mrs Craik), *Nothing New* (1861). The latter, which first appeared in the pages of *Once a Week*, were reprinted to advantage in 1865 (Book Illustrations 30).

14 Mason 1978, p.309. He continues: 'In all other cases where an artist illustrated several works by a novelist these were wholly or in part reissues (as with Du Maurier's illustrations to Mrs Gaskell).'

a significant observation, and it goes some way towards explaining the continuing (and entirely valid) interest in Trollope and Millais's work for his novels. Yet Millais had so much to offer both intellectually and stylistically when called upon to draw for other contemporary writers such as Harriet Martineau, Mrs Craik (Dinah Mulock), Tennyson and others, as well as for texts where the authors were long dead. An example of the latter can be found in the *Arabian Nights' Entertainments* of 1865.

So Millais could draw both for new and reprinted literature, and for a number of literary genres. He was immensely versatile in that he could alter his style in order to do justice to the text before him. Is it possible then to attempt to define and examine some of these various styles and identify and isolate his use of motifs, poses, and expressions within these various modes?

First, for texts based on history or antiquity he drew with deep feeling in an 'antiquarian' style: for poems from Norse mythology, several of which appeared in the first years of *Once a Week*, as well as for the stories of Harriet Martineau in the same organ, which were set, for example at the time of Monmouth's Rebellion.[15] In each case Millais took care to render the costume of the period in a manner that is accurate, appropriate and invariably sensitive. Similarly, in the Moxon Tennyson of 1857 it is possible to see him using both this style and a contrasting 'modern' one in the same
74 volume. For example, 'A Dream of Fair Women' (page 161) is a crowded scene where we read:

> Or her, who knew that Love can vanquish Death,
> Who kneeling, with one arm about her king,
> Drew forth the poison with her balmy breath,
> Sweet as new buds in Spring.

Here the atmosphere is one of a suffocating mediaeval interior and undeniable melodrama, and yet many pages later comes 'Edward Gray' where on
77 page 340 are figures in contemporary dress and, more significantly still, rendered in a deliberately modern manner.

The Pre-Raphaelites favoured the device of two figures turned uncomfortably and seen from behind to suggest inner conflict. Millais, though, also uses the single figure on numerous occasions to depict emotion; examples of this can be detected throughout his work. In 'A Dream of Fair Women', on
74 page 149 of the Moxon Tennyson, is a single figure (Cleopatra) tearing open
72 her clothing to reveal the snake bite; on page seven in 'Mariana', a poem set somewhat later, the isolated figure bent double with despair becomes almost an abstract shape. Hence Millais, with texts set in almost any period, can draw in a manner which is direct and often disconcertingly up-to-date. Moreover, stylistically there are yet further refinements to be mentioned. While the 'Dream of Fair Women' design just mentioned is a dark and richly worked image, he also frequently employed a more summary, even sketchy style. A typical example is 'Maude Clare', a poem by Christina Rossetti

15 'Son Christopher', *Once a Week*, 24 October – 12 December 1863. See Periodical Illustrations 9:lx–lxvii.

which appeared in *Once a Week* on 5 November 1859. As is so often the case, 265
it is not transparently clear exactly where Millais is laying his stress – but he seems to illustrate lines from the second verse:

> She follow'd his bride into the church,
> With a lofty step and mien:
> His bride was like a village maid,
> Maude Clare was like a queen.

For this drawing Millais uses a number of swiftly executed strokes especially on clothing, while rendering faces in a sort of shorthand, with a series of either horizontal or vertical lines. In the hands of a lesser artist this device might look rough, scratched, even careless; however, to me the sketchiness endows the lines with a vigour and a vivacity which bring the scene to life. This was a technique that Millais resorted to frequently, especially in the designs for this periodical, and on many occasions, though not all, it seems to suit the text very well.

In complete contrast, Millais sometimes employs a style which is meticulously worked up and concentrated. A typical example is the frontispiece
called 'Cosette' for Victor Hugo's *Les Misérables*.[16] While allowing for 140
more detail inherent in Saddler's immaculate steel-engraving technique, there is also a depth of feeling and a sense of dappled light falling on the dress that only Millais with his gossamer touch can provide. It is one of his loveliest and most direct designs for illustration: indeed, as a group his drawings for the frontispieces in the Hurst and Blackett *Standard Library* Series are invariably rewarding. The image in question leads on to two other facets of Millais's illustrative style – his drawing of women and his use of the single figure.

As an illustrator of women Millais shows a mastery not merely of costume but also of pose and emotion. Hugo writes, 'she tried to turn her eyes away from these pages which trembled in her hand'.[17] Millais does not simply give us a portrait but, I would venture, something deeper – a motionless character at the same time intent, concentrating and alive. In addition there is the single figure, itself a subject of convention, yet here and on numerous other occasions Millais makes this figure a monumental and central one. The billowing skirt suggests not only a fully formed, breathing woman but, more significantly, a rounded human being. So Millais was a fine draughtsman of women whose achievements exceed mere facility in draughtsmanship. He had a subtle ability to suggest emotion, reality and character by means of the single figure, frequently female. He must have been well aware that many (perhaps a majority) of his readers were themselves women, hence by depicting the sex in a credible and truthful manner he would be able to retain their interest and attention.

On other occasions Millais draws women who are not wearing crinolines, evidently from a less exalted social class. One of the most memorable

16 Engraved by John Saddler. Other examples in a similar manner are the frontispieces for *The Valley of a Hundred Fires* and *Mistress and Maid*, both in the Hurst and Blackett *Standard Library* (Book Illustrations 24, 14 and 17).
17 P.319 lines 8–9.

265 of these appears in 'The Plague of Elliant', in which a sorrowing mother pulls the bodies of her dead children on a cart. It is a sight of pain and heartbreak, yet one rendered with a strength, even a grandeur, redolent of some of the Barbizon School etchers, notably Millet.[18]

Millais also made a strong point in drawing scenes with just two figures, of which several of the most powerful occur in *The Parables of Our Lord*
156 (1864). Two celebrated examples are 'The Prodigal Son' and 'The Good
151 Samaritan'. These are dramatic scenes, yet the figures are in harmony, not conflict: in the former the supreme emotion is forgiveness and in the latter it might be called compassion. Millais uses very natural poses, and by so doing removes the scene from the remote past to make what is going on understandable, and in a curious way contemporary and immediate. The presence of the animals in Scottish surroundings[19] domesticates the images and brings them down to earth and within the compass of the mid-Victorian reader. Nevertheless, there is no lack of dignity or gravity in these designs, for the artist has invested each of them with the most profound and delicate emotion. It is possible, I think, without being naïve or crass, to see in 'The Good Samaritan' a totally human response of one man comforting another after the latter has been beaten up – 'mugged'.

A useful comparison may be made with the Parable designs and the other great biblical enterprise of the period, *Dalziel's Bible Gallery*. This extraordinary production did not reach publication until many years later but it was planned at almost the same time as Millais was working on the Parables.[20] Tellingly, Millais made no contributions at all to this work – while his Parables are domestic in scale yet profound in their feeling, the majority of the *Bible Gallery* drawings are on an epic canvas showing the characters from the Old Testament as remote, titanic and overwhelming. In examples such as Edward Poynter's 'Moses slaying the Egyptian' or 'Jacob blessing Ephraim and Manasseh' by Frederick Richard Pickersgill, where the figures are depicted in fine style but relatively conventionally, they are unapproachable and the world they inhabit is very clearly the Holy Land of thousands of years ago.

Millais could also draw the two-figure configuration in a more domestic setting and excelled in depicting lovers, both of the enraptured and the
264 tortured variety. An example of the former is 'On the Water' and of the
82 latter the justly celebrated 'Love'.[21] While the feeling in each design is one of desire, the atmosphere and the handling are utterly different. 'On the Water' suggests a gentle, peaceful contentment, which is echoed in the silent gliding of the boat through the still water. 'Love', in complete contrast, reveals a strength of passion which is disturbing and overwrought. The two forms are

18 *Once A Week*, 15 October 1859, p.316, Periodical Illustrations 9:v. See for example and comparison J. F. Millet, 'Les Glaneuses' (The Gleaners), etching, 1855/6. It is likely that Millais knew the work of Millet and his contemporaries, as both his paintings and prints were collected and admired in England at this period.

19 The scene is at his wife Effie's family house, Bowerswell, Perth.

20 *Dalziel's Bible Gallery*, London: Routledge, 1881 (actually published in October 1880). Engravings after Frederic Leighton, Simeon Solomon, Holman Hunt, Burne-Jones, etc.

21 *Once a Week*, 23 July 1859, p.70, Periodical Illustrations 9:iii; R.A. Willmott (ed.), *The Poets of the Nineteenth Century* (Book Illustrations 7), p.137.

intertwined in an embrace of overwhelming emotion, which reflects almost in mirror image the love expressed in the poem. Forrest Reid, never a critic to overpraise, felt impelled to exclaim of the design that it was '... in no way inferior to the work of Coleridge himself'.[22]

Another area which is worthy of examination is Millais's treatment of children and, more especially, of girls. He seems invariably sympathetic and tender to such figures but rarely sentimental. He drew with care for books clearly intended for children and also managed to provide credible youthful characters in his illustrations for a more adult readership. There is an essential difference between drawing children for children and in depicting them for their parents.

It may perhaps be a truism to remark that this was a period of high infant mortality but there is an undoubted link between so constant a preoccupation and the frequent appearance of children in illustration. On occasion certain artists strayed over the border from 'sentiment' into 'sentimentality', yet this is an accusation that can rarely be levelled at Millais.[23] When he draws specifically for children he seems entirely at home in their world. For example, in a design such as 'Our Sister Grizel' (Sarah Tytler [Henrietta Keddie], *Papers for Thoughtful Girls* [1863]), Millais provides a scene with 136
which the children for whom the book was intended could identify and enjoy. Unusually there is a boy in this image, but Millais almost always excels more with the female form at whatever age. His young boys often appear like this one – somewhat stiff and priggish.

When a child appears in a work more directly aimed at adults, it seems to me that there is sometimes a subtle difference in handling: here it seems somewhat graver and heavier in feeling. An example is 'The Grandmother's Apology' in *Once a Week*, where the young girl sits at her grandmother's feet in a pose that is natural but essentially pensive.[24] This superb design 263
shows Millais's ability to depict old age with truthful intensity; indeed, the juxtaposition between youth and age is a favourite and a recurrent motif in Victorian illustration. This again suggests that such a theme came about because death was ever-present in a way that is difficult to comprehend now. It is no coincidence that the Victorians placed so great an emphasis on mourning and the conduct of funerals. The poignant link between the girl and her grandmother is rich with tender care, and Millais eloquently echoes Tennyson's lines telling of the death of the old woman's eldest son. She looks back on her life and muses to her granddaughter:

> So Willy has gone, my beauty, my eldest-born, my flower;
> But how can I weep for Willy, he has but gone for an hour, –
> Gone for a minute, my son, from this room into the next;
> I, too, shall go in a minute. What time have I to be vext?

22 *Illustrators of the Sixties*, London: Faber and Gwyer, 1928, p.67.
23 For an example of an overtly sentimental view of children in illustration at this period see *Pictures of English Life ... with descriptive poems by J. G. Watts*, London: Sampson Low, Son and Marston, 1865. Arguably the masterpiece in illustration by Robert Barnes (1840–1895), designs such as 'The Sick Child' may well be seen as somewhat cloying today.
24 1859, p.41, Periodical Illustrations 9:ii.

This design also highlights the care Millais invariably takes over facial aspect. Although the viewer can barely perceive the expression on the little girl's face, that of the old woman is, with the fewest of strokes, depicted with all its crow's-feet of resigned stoicism.

There are numerous other examples warranting similar examination: two of the most remarkable were made once again for a Tennyson poem, 'Saint
78 Agnes' Eve'. The first occurs in the Moxon Tennyson of 1857 and the second
185 in a little noticed book of 1883, Henry Leslie's *Songs for Little Folks*.[25] Once
more there is a delineation of youth and age. The earlier design shows a young novice gazing out over the snow, her breath visibly vapourising in the frosty air; later we have a more mature woman, clearly a nun, seen in profile this time but with the selfsame motif expertly realised:

> Deep on the convent-roof the snows
> Are sparkling to the moon:
> My breath to heaven like vapour goes:
> May my soul follow soon!

While the youthful figure is clad from head to toe in white, as a newly empassioned bride of Christ and a long way off from death, the older figure by contrast has, in her expression, a feeling of the approach of mortality. In the earlier drawing there is to my eyes a sense of spiritual rapture, almost excitement, while in the latter the atmosphere conveyed by the face is more one of readiness to depart this life.

It is in the novels, especially those by Trollope, that we find several of the finest examples of Millais's handling of group scenes. The group is never an easy subject to bring off in the cramped surroundings offered by a page, but to my mind several of the best are in *Orley Farm*. In, for example, 'There is
96 nothing like iron, Sir; nothing' there is the amusing sight of the ridiculous Mr
Kantwise demonstrating the strength of the iron furniture he is trying to peddle by balancing on top of the table and performing a sort of jig on it. Millais sees the risible in the scene and interprets it to the letter, ensuring that this predecessor of Mr Pooter actually does wave his arms above his head as Trollope requires. The throng of 'admirers' is also neatly depicted, their poses and expressions reflecting various emotions – incredulity, irritation and downright boredom. This drawing is unusual in that it is clearly intentionally funny: Millais can easily handle humour but it would be incorrect to see this aspect as one which looms large in his illustrated work.

Another, smaller group of just three figures from *The Small House at*
223 *Allington* is also successfully brought off. This is 'The Board', which has
been convened to ascertain whether Adolphus Crosbie is suitable for Civil Service promotion. Once more Millais draws the scene as stipulated by Trollope. That old bore, Sir Raffle Buffle, is really standing with 'his back to the fire-place, talking very loudly'. What Millais has encapsulated so well is the dry and grey nature of this scene in the Ministry. How wonderfully has

25 The frontispiece design was almost certainly made at about the same time as the Moxon Tennyson drawings but inexplicably held over until its belated appearance in a children's book. This volume is essentially a reprint of *Little Songs for me to Sing* (1865) by the same author. The frontispiece appears nowhere else in Millais's oeuvre. Book Illustrations 63.

he captured Mr Optimist, the heir to Buffle's chairmanship, 'standing behind the armchair, rubbing his hands together, and longing for the departure of Sir Raffle, in order that he might sit down'. Optimist looks for all the world exactly what he is – a small-time official crawling up the greasy pole, fixing the incoming candidate with a glassy stare through his spectacles.[26]

While it cannot be said with truthfulness that Millais is greatly interested in landscape in illustration, there are instances where he takes particular care to render a setting to strengthen the dramatic sense. Some of the most telling
examples occur in *The Parables of Our Lord*. In 'The Parable of the Lost 154
Sheep' the tale is given an additional dimension with the lost animal being recovered only a short distance from the edge of a beetling cliff, with an
eagle circling above, cheated of its prey.[27] Similarly, in 'The Prodigal Son' 156
there is perhaps a pond in the foreground, with two unconcerned sheep and a curious barn with a conical roof in the background.[28] The earth-shattering moment of the Parable itself contrasts profoundly with the everyday nature of Millais's landscape. It is this very 'matter-of-factness' which strengthens and clarifies the meaning of the Parable itself by making it immediate and crystal clear to the reader and to the viewer.

Does Millais invariably choose the most obviously 'dramatic' moment in a story or a poem on which to base his drawing? Examination of them all suggests that this is not inevitably the case. In the novels in particular he frequently hinges a design on dialogue or the interrogative. For example, in
Orley Farm there are images entitled 'Tell me, Madelaine, are you happy 122
now?' and 'And how are they all at Noningsby?', yet in the same novel we 127
also find illustrations which are essentially scene-setting rather than moments of genuine drama.

In 'The Drawing-room at Noningsby' and 'Mr. Chaffanbrass and Mr. 126
Solomon Aram', both episodes of some significance in moving the narrative 124
onward, there is, if truth be told, little in the way of real tension or excitement. Whether this is a matter for adverse criticism of the illustrator is open to dispute, for it could be argued that to concentrate solely on dramatic incidents might reduce the impact of the text. What it does show, in my view, is that Millais is a more careful and sentient illustrator than previously given credit. There is a complexity about his work in illustration that reveals a thoughtful approach and occasionally even an inspired one.

Nevertheless, it is not altogether a story of total success: in some of the most lauded of the Trollope novels, Millais appears bored and even routine in his approach. *Phineas Finn, The Irish Member*, arguably one of the most penetrating and cogent of Trollope's political novels, appears to have failed
to inspire Millais to the heights of imagination. For example, in 'Laura, 319
would you mind leaving me and Miss Effingham alone for a few minutes?' the scene is conventional in the extreme, and the facial expressions flaccid
and unconvincing. Similarly, even in 'I wish to regard you as a dear friend, 318

26 For a penetrating study of these particular designs see Hall 1980, pp.69ff.

27 The landscape in 'The Parable of the Lost Sheep' is borrowed from Holman Hunt's 'Our English Coasts: Strayed Sheep', 1852, Tate Britain.

28 Robin de Beaumont recalls seeing this building at Bowerswell (possibly a dovecote) in the late 1960s.

both of my own and of my husband', where Finn realises with incredulity that the delectable Lady Laura has chosen Mr Kennedy instead of himself – a moment of pure drama if ever there was one – Millais falls short: the figures are wooden, the poses dull and the features stylised. So Millais is not invariably *hors de concours* as an illustrator. Nevertheless, for the most part he has more to say and he says it more lucidly than the majority of his rivals. Rossetti was wayward and esoteric but he produced so little; the same might be said of Ford Madox Brown, Holman Hunt and Burne-Jones, considered purely as illustrators.

In terms of output and range a more useful comparison might be made with Arthur Boyd Houghton who, like Millais, was a prolific master of many types of illustration. Houghton had moments of sheer inspiration, not least in an extraordinary book containing some of the most disturbing images of childhood in the whole history of illustration.[28] Yet Houghton rarely obtained similar commissions to Millais, where he was given the opportunity to illustrate entire works single-handed, and certainly never enjoyed a working relationship with a novelist of the calibre of Trollope. Too many of his superb designs are scattered in relatively minor books and periodicals and, in one area in particular, he could not approach Millais. As an illustrator of children for adults, Houghton was outstanding; yet when he tried to draw for the juvenile market he appeared to lack the ability to alter his style as Millais did so well.[29]

Millais, then, is an illustrator of many strengths and few weaknesses. Above all, he understood instinctively the importance of the 'moment' in illustration and possessed an almost unerring eye for the one that he could enhance, illuminate and clarify.

28 *Home Thoughts and Home Scenes in Original Poems*, London: Routledge, Warne and Routledge, 1865. Thirty-five designs engraved by Dalziel after Houghton.
29 See for example Elizabeth Eiloart, *Ernie Elton, The Lazy Boy*, London: Routledge, 1865 and *Ernie at School and What came of his Going There*, London: Routledge, 1867.

CHAPTER TWO

The Book Illustrations

WHILE MILLAIS MAY NOT BE CONSIDERED prolific in terms of numbers of book illustration designs, especially if he is compared with such successors as William Heath Robinson or Arthur Rackham, he was undoubtedly their equal if not their superior in the width of his compass. It is, therefore, useful to categorise the various areas of book design into which he ventured.

First, it is worthwhile to attempt to differentiate between new and reprinted literature. For example, Wilkie Collins's *Mr. Wray's Cash-Box*, Allingham's *The Music Master* and Trollope's *Orley Farm* are all genuine first editions; this is significant because, almost inevitably, there is likely to have been some communication between author and illustrator. In the case of Trollope this relationship has been extensively explored and documented.[1] Where the artist contributed to reprinted texts a similar such interaction is far less likely, and where the author was not alive there is no such issue to consider, as in *The Parables of Our Lord* or *Dalziel's Illustrated Arabian Nights Entertainments*. Nevertheless, where the text was recently reprinted and the author still alive there is at least the possibility of some author and illustrator link. Among such volumes are Tennyson's *Poems* of 1857 (the Moxon Tennyson) and Dinah Mulock (Mrs Craik), *John Halifax, Gentleman* (1861). It is well known that Tennyson was very little interested in illustrations to his own poems. According to Forrest Reid,

> Tennyson, rather oddly, since after all they were *his* poems, took less interest in the matter than anybody else – so little indeed that he seems to have expressed no desire to even look at the drawings till they were, in some cases, already cut on the wood.
>
> To him, apparently, all were equally unimportant. If the public wanted them they should have them, but the pictures that mattered were those in the mind's eye which his own art evoked.[2]

It is difficult to know whether there was any real dialogue between Millais and Mulock or, indeed, any other contemporaries such as Julia Stretton, for whom he provided drawings. Where he contributed merely a single design

1 Hall 1980; Mason 1978.
2 *Illustrators of the Sixties*, p.43.

such as a frontispiece, it seems more than likely that any communication between author and illustrator would have been minimal.

In terms of literary categories, Millais drew for both contemporary novels and verse written primarily for adults. In addition, he designed for Trollope and Collins who were writing about their own times, for Mulock and Thackeray who were contemporaries, but whose relevant books were historical, and for earlier writers such as Defoe.[3] Such a range hints at a remarkable ability to relate to literature of several types. Turning specifically to poetry, once again the variety to be found is somewhat greater than might be expected. While Allingham and Tennyson were contemporaries, Thomas Moore[4] had penned his *Irish Melodies* between 1807 and 1834 and had been dead for several years before Millais turned his attention to the work.[5] Similarly, in the anthologies Millais regularly illustrated the work of earlier poets.[6] In *Lays of the Holy Land* he produced a single drawing for a religious poem by James
84 Grahame (1765–1811) called 'Moses on the Nile': here he alters his style once
again to match the rapt and spiritual nature of the lines

> And wakes the infant, smiling in his tears, –
> As when along a little mountain lake,
> The summer south-wind breathes with gentle sigh,
> And parts the reeds, unveiling, as they bend,
> A water-lily floating on the wave.

The sense of concentration and enchantment on the girls' faces immeasurably strengthens the frankly rather vapid verse. Then in Charles Mackay's collection *The Home Affections Pourtrayed by the Poets*, Millais turns his
88 attention to a tough anonymous ballad, 'The Border Widow', and powerful-
ly evokes the despair after a battle. We can see, without compromise, the discarded sword and helmet and the burning buildings in the background. In a tiny space he makes a potent comment not just about the text, but also about the nature of war itself. In Henry Leslie's charming *Little Songs for Me to Sing* Millais is called upon to draw for a book that is at the same time a volume of children's verse and a book of music, destined to do duty on a music stand.[7] This is hence a rewarding and a somewhat more complex book
169 than has previously been viewed. The first verse of 'The Sweet Story of Old'
reads as follows:

> I THINK, when I read that sweet story of old,
> When Jesus dwelt here among men;
> And call'd little children as lambs to his fold,
> I should like to have been with them then.

3 For Thackeray see *The Memoirs of Barry Lyndon, Esq.*, 1879; for Defoe, *Robinson Crusoe*, 1866.

4 This is one of a group of drawings made in 1853–4 of subjects from contemporary life. See *The Drawings of John Everett Millais*, exh. cat., Arts Council of Great Britain, 1979, no.21, p.22.

5 *Irish Melodies*, London: Longman, 1856.

6 For example in R.A. Willmott, *The Poets of the Nineteenth Century*, 1857, Millais illustrated poems by Byron and Coleridge.

7 It is a fragile volume and is bound by having the heavy card leaves glued to the spine rather than sewn in a technique today euphemistically referred to as 'Perfect Binding'. The Victorians made extensive use of a kind of latex called 'Gutta-percha' which quickly perished. It is for this reason that so many of the books of the mid-nineteenth century thus bound lack one or more illustrations because the method of binding ensured that pages rapidly became loose.

For this less than outstanding verse Millais produces a striking, unsentimental drawing of a little girl intently reading. The motif of children reading was one to which he returned on several occasions.

In 1863 he had made the tiny title-page vignette of a similar subject for
Wordsworth's Poems for the Young, but arguably the finest and most 139
moving treatment is the large title-page design for *Millais's Collected Illus-* 175
trations which appeared in 1866. Here again are two little girls reading, the one on the left tracing the words with her fingers. A discarded doll is flung aside in the foreground, while behind is a somewhat awkward woman bending to a task, with just the suggestion of a landscape glimpsed through the window beyond. Next to the girls is an artist's palette. The children appear to be seated before an easel and are raised, as if on a model's platform. The harmony of the two figures pressing close in order to better follow the text might perhaps be seen as Millais expressing his feelings as regards illustration. While the idea is admittedly somewhat fanciful, it is true to say that in this rather overlooked design several of Millais's finest attributes as an illustrator are manifest: the strong, central motif of the two figures – the modelling, especially of the hair, the clothing and the legs; the masterly drawing of the features and the hands; and overall, the overwhelming sense of the vivacity of the little protagonists. It would be so very easy to slip into mawkishness here, but I believe that Millais resists the temptation, producing a timeless image.

Not all areas of design suited Millais: he rarely seems at home with the
foreign or the exotic. In Dalziel's *Arabian Nights' Entertainments* of 1865, 164
neither of the artist's two contributions is outstanding. While both are 165
decently drawn, Millais does not convey anything of the heady mix of the lubricious and the mystic which these tales demand. Instead it was left to Arthur Boyd Houghton, who provided the majority of the designs, to make it his own and a triumph, albeit a flawed one.[8]

While it is invariably preferable to see Millais's designs in the settings for which they were intended, with the text alongside or in close proximity, there is a number of collections of designs that prove handy compilations. The *Collected Illustrations* already mentioned are of especial interest because of the choice of contents. The selection appears to be arbitrary, presumably made by the publisher Alexander Strahan and hence limited to material to which he could readily obtain access. The order makes no sense whatever and as a display of the range of the artist's skills as a draughtsman it is deficient. Nevertheless, this and the various other anthologies have an interest worthy of investigation.

Perhaps most obviously, these books were almost invariably printed on better paper than the designs had originally been accorded, especially in the magazines. The impressions were occasionally pulled from the original boxwood blocks:[9] although this is rarely stated in the books themselves, greater care taken in the printing makes it possible to see the designs in the

8 See Paul Hogarth, *Arthur Boyd Houghton*, London: Gordon Fraser, 1981; Reid 1928, p.195.
9 In the *Cornhill Gallery* it is stated that the designs are printed from the wood. However, no such declaration is made in the *Collected Illustrations* of 1866. The designs are simply termed 'A Collection of Drawings on Wood'.

clearest manner. It is instructive to see Millais's works in a compilation such as *The Cornhill Gallery* (1864), cheek by jowl with the products of the other leading illustrators of the day. This tells us something about the position of Millais in the artistic world of the time. Out of the hundred designs here Millais contributed twenty-nine – a considerable proportion by any yardstick. Yet further it may be said that anthologies of this type are essentially 'Art Books', in the sense that they were created wholly to highlight the skill of the artist and engraver – the illustrations are removed from their settings and the text is of little or no significance in such a context.

The lavish and luxurious nature of such books of pictures – indeed, their very existence – points to a market for them, as well as suggesting that illustration at the time was viewed with interest by a public that could afford to purchase an early and relatively unsophisticated form of *livre d'artiste*. A comparison might be made with the manner in which proof engravings from steel-engraved books were marketed by publishers some twenty or thirty years earlier. For example, at the back of *The Amulet – A Christian and Literary Remembrancer* for 1830 there is an advertisement for 'Proofs of the Amulet Illustrations'. These could be purchased separately from the volume and at a higher price: 'Proofs, unlettered (set, in a portfolio) £2 10s. Proofs, lettered (ditto) £1. 10s'. As far as I am aware, the publishers of wood-engraved books of the later period did not often issue equivalent portfolios of proofs, but by producing anthologies of illustration they were doing something not entirely dissimilar.[10] They were also attempting to raise the status of wood-engraving as a fine art by dignifying their images in this way.[11]

The books containing etchings by Millais belong to the same category and are little more than folders of designs produced for artistic rather than literary considerations. They are books in name only with minimal accompanying texts. Fine as they undoubtedly are as specimens of print-making, they are scarcely illustrations in the sense that I believe most of his other designs should be viewed. These volumes look both backwards to the Annuals of the 1820s and 1830s just mentioned, and forward to the twentieth century concept of 'Book Art' where the book becomes a work of art – an item to be handled with gloves and put into a display cabinet. Unsurprisingly, many of these books of etchings have been dismantled and the prints removed for framing. The format of such volumes tacitly encourages such a practice, whereas the collected volumes of wood-engravings are frequently complete: if images are missing it is more likely because of collapse of the binding rather than deliberate removal. It seems that despite the best efforts of Dalziel and Alexander Strahan to raise the status of wood-engraving to a more exalted and respected level, it would not be until the next century that wood-engraving could break through the barrier to full artistic respectability. This may well have come about because at this later

10 The De Luxe version of the *Bible Gallery*, 1881, was an exception since it is made up of separate prints loose in a portfolio.

11 A further exception to this rule is *Twenty-Nine Illustrations by John Everett Millais designed for the Cornhill Magazine* of 1867. However, although these are proofs I can find no evidence to suggest that it was ever possible to purchase them individually from the publisher, Smith Elder.

date the artist and engraver became one and the same, so the position of the artist-engraver was enhanced in the mind of the collector and amateur.[12]

Although the initial twelve designs of *The Parables of Our Lord* appeared in *Good Words* in 1863, the project reached complete book publication in 1864. It is a remarkable work for several reasons, some of which are discussed above (pp.16,19).[13] For some critics it marks the zenith of Millais's achievement as an illustrator, while others view it with more caution. On its first appearance it provoked some widely differing reactions. One commentator wrote:

> no one can justly deny that he [Millais] brings to his work an earnest, thoughtful and reverential mind, a truly poetical imagination, and a thorough knowledge of the technicalities of Art; his feelings, so far as relates to the spirit of his compositions, are in perfect harmony with the old Italian painters who preceded Raffaelle, and which we could desire that others of our artists who attempt sacred art exhibited to a greater extent than they do, yet without adopting implicitly their antique manner as models.... There is not one of these subjects which does not stand out in striking and noble contrast with the prettiness and sentimentalism that too frequently characterises the works purporting to express sacred art, and which are so often mistaken for it.[14]

In complete contrast came a more probing comment:

> Although it is true that many of the designs before us are really trivial, and show little of a deep conception of the subject, it is also true that the majority possess high qualities of Art.... The force of treatment in "The Pharisee and the Publican" gives it the power of an oil painting. These are rare qualities of execution in which Mr. Millais excels when he does himself justice.... When, however, we look for signs of a comprehensive pre-consideration of the method in which such a series of subjects should be treated, disappointment faces us.[15]

Some years later the critical balance had shifted to a heartfelt admiration not just for the *Parables*, but for Millais's illustrative work as a whole:

> From them [Millais's illustrations] one learns that he had seen and enjoyed and been strengthened by the great illustrators of the past; that he was willing to profit by the methods discovered by his immediate predecessors and contemporaries – Gigoux, the Johannots, Meissonier, John Gilbert – to produce a series of drawings, which, if so trivial a detail is worth consideration, are thoroughly English. Far more important, they are thoroughly artistic... [of the *Parables*] ... in these there is the same conviction and realism that one finds in Rembrandt and the old men.... If Rossetti resurrected the Pre-Raphaelite method of drawing; if Frederick Sandys brought it to perfection; at the same time, Millais explained, most conclusively, that the life around us is as beautiful as anything in the past ... with him, this form of art was developed.[16]

In the light of these words of J. and E. R. Pennell, it is perhaps unsurprising

12 For a comprehensive study of the later period see Joanna Selborne, *British Wood-Engraved Book Illustration 1904–1940*, Oxford: Clarendon Press, 1998.

13 Leonard Roberts has pointed out the existence of the following book that reprints a single Parable illustration. It is Thomas Guthrie, *The Parables: Read in the Light of the Present Day*, London: Alexander Strahan, 1866. The frontispiece is a reprint of 'The Parable of the Virgin', here entitled 'The Ten Virgins', first published in *Good Words* in 1863, facing p. 81.

14 *Art Journal*, February 1864, p.59. Unsigned review.

15 *Athenaeum*, no.1887, 26 December 1863, pp.881–2. Unsigned review.

16 Pennell 1896, pp.443–50.

that Gleeson White was able to write in his pioneering study, published just a few months later, in a manner which recognised in full and without hyperbole the artist's unique contribution to illustration. White remarked on the *Parables*:

> It is difficult to write dispassionately of this book. Granted that when you compare it with the drawings of some of the subjects which are still extant, you regret certain shortcomings on the part of the engravers; yet when studied apart from that severe test, there is much that is not merely the finest work of a fine period, but that may be placed among the finest of any period.... If any one who loves art, especially the art of illustration, does not know and prize these *Parables*, then it were foolish to add a line in their praise, for ignorance of such masterpieces is criminal, and lukewarm approval a fatal confession.[17]

In view of the quality and variety of Millais's contributions to books it seems inexplicable that so few of his designs were reprinted in later editions during the ensuing hundred and forty years.[18]

As a book illustrator Millais displays a myriad of talents both technical and artistic. His variety and range cannot be disputed; within the books are to be found some of his most profound and serious thoughts and sensibilities. Three works in particular encapsulate his skill: the Moxon Tennyson, *The Parables of Our Lord* and *Orley Farm*. Each in its own way demonstrates more than mere ability. In the Tennyson, there is a mix of styles 'ancient' and 'modern' so complete as to be utterly arresting. The *Parables* are some of the most reverent and spiritual treatments of the subject in all art, while the Trollope drawings are of such a quality that they genuinely enhance and expand our understanding of one of the author's gravest utterances on human weakness.

17 Gleeson White, *English Illustration: The Sixties 1855–70*, London: Constable and Co., 1897, pp.119–20.
18 A notable exception is the reprint of *The Parables of Our Lord* with a new introduction by Mary Lutyens, 1975.

CHAPTER THREE

The Periodical Illustrations

MILLAIS MADE ILLUSTRATIONS FOR NINE periodicals, although in terms of the range of his contributions only four of these can really be considered of genuine importance: *The Cornhill Magazine*, *Good Words*, *Once a Week* and *Saint Pauls*.[1]

The periodicals as a whole are awkward and inconvenient to deal with. First, and most obviously, there is the daunting nature of their sheer bulk – the prospect of wading through acres of close-set type, only occasionally relieved by an illustration, can dismay even the most assiduous and enthusiastic researcher. This coupled with poor paper and shoddy printing can also be depressing and enervating and it is perhaps for these reasons that Forrest Reid, like many early critics, recommended drastic action:

> The magazines present a difficult problem. They are essential to a collection that pretends to any degree of completeness but on the other hand they take up a good deal of room, and it is extremely tedious to have to turn over several hundred pages for the sake of perhaps a dozen, perhaps only two or three, drawings. To those whose shelf room is limited the temptation to extract the prints worth extracting becomes almost irresistible, and as far as the collector himself is concerned this course is undoubtedly the more satisfactory. Not only will he be able to classify his drawings, but the drawings themselves will look much better when mounted separately on white boards than when wedged between unattractive slabs of letterpress. The margin of the board supplies at once a foil to the tint of the paper and a frame, showing the whole picture to the best advantage.
>
> Yet, to mutilate a volume of *The Cornhill* or *Good Words* is an act of vandalism, to say nothing of the really rare magazines.
>
> In the case of a magazine like *Good Words for the Young* it is hoped that nobody will think of doing so, any more than of cutting up a volume of *Punch*. After all, the original setting has an interest of its own, and as time passes this interest increases.[2]

Forrest Reid's final line is the crucial one: despite his appeal against vandalism, he succumbed to the very temptation himself and innumerable other collectors followed his advice almost to the letter. He cut his own collection of periodical designs from the issues, mounted and annotated each one impeccably and he

1 Despite references elsewhere to the magazine as *St. Paul's*, its title was *Saint Pauls*.
2 Reid 1928, p.11.

eventually presented the group, boxed neatly and admittedly easy to use, to the Ashmolean Museum in Oxford. Several further collections, identically organised, are now in other museums.[3]

The consequences of the wholesale destruction of so many periodical runs are only today becoming fully appreciated. Unbroken sets of the magazines are rare and, even where they have been retained in libraries, are frequently in poor condition. Pages (including those with illustrations) have sometimes been crudely laminated, which means that detail and quality can barely be perceived. In addition, the bound volumes hardly ever retain their informative wrappers that regularly carry invaluable information as to issue and date, as well as advertisements sometimes for related magazines and books. Indeed it is sometimes difficult to work out the exact month an issue appeared because such information only appeared on the wrapper and not within the body of the periodical. Also, these library runs almost invariably omit special issues such as those printed at Christmas and Holiday time. This means that certain illustrations can prove elusive and difficult to examine and study.

If the magazines present so many problems, should not the researcher simply note their existence and concentrate on the books instead? It is a reaction to be resisted, since the periodicals are of genuine significance for a number of reasons. First, and perhaps a little obviously, it is worth remarking that the literature is, almost without exception, new, while several of the books, in contrast, are little more than reprints. Hence it is possible to view Millais's contributions to the periodicals in a special light: he is responding here to contemporary writing in a spontaneous and, of necessity on occasion, a speedy manner. Apparent in several of these designs is a haste that can sometimes look shoddy but is, at the same time, immediate, lively and vivacious. I have already mentioned an example of such a design in the first chapter (pp.14–15), but there are several others that deserve note. In addition, since Millais contributed to several magazines, each with its own characteristics, we have the opportunity to appreciate his illustrations in all their variety of style and approach. The sheer quality and distinction of much of his work here can still be perceived despite the negative properties mentioned above, most disturbingly decomposing paper and dull printing.

There is one further and more practical point to be mentioned in favour of the periodicals. Sometimes when a novel that first appeared in a magazine was reprinted in book form, its appearance underwent subtle changes. This regularly went well beyond simple resetting and using a different paper stock, and when it came to illustrations a cavalier attitude was not unusual. An instructive example is *The Small House at Allington*, where the first book edition omits not only the illustration included with the twentieth periodical instalment, but also all the delightful initial-letter vignettes that begin each chapter so tellingly.

Thus the primacy of the 'First Printing' over the 'First Edition' is transparently more than mere academic nicety. The advantages of better production must be weighed against those of the completeness of utterance to be found in the periodicals. Illustrations reprinted in book form from periodicals sometimes

3 See Paul Goldman and Brian Taylor (eds), *Retrospective Adventures – Forrest Reid: Author and Collector*, Aldershot: Scolar Press and Oxford: Ashmolean Museum, 1998.

suffer such indignities as reduction or cropping, so once again the case for invariably going initially to periodical issues in connection with illustration is strengthened.

It is worth looking at some of these periodicals individually to examine their particular viewpoints and characteristics, and to investigate the manner in which Millais adapted to meet them. The *Cornhill* was arguably the most weighty and intellectual of all the magazines with which Millais was involved. Edited at the outset in 1860 by Thackeray, it immediately attracted major novelists and poets including Trollope, George Eliot, Mrs Gaskell and Elizabeth Barrett Browning. The first volume (January to June 1860) contains *Framley Parsonage*, *Lovel the Widower* which was both written and illustrated by the editor, and poetic contributions from Thomas Hood, Richard Monckton Milnes, Tennyson ('Tithonus') and a work by the long-deceased Emily Brontë.[4] It was into this heady milieu that Millais plunged, and some of his finest Trollope designs appear here – first to 'Framley Parsonage' and a little later to 'The Small House at Allington'.[5] Interspersed with the Trollope drawings are one or two fine
things that are easy to overlook. That to 'Unspoken Dialogue' (February 1860; 198
Periodical Illustrations 4:i) is particularly noteworthy, for it is both Millais's first contribution to the *Cornhill* and also one of his tenderest. The comparison between youth and experience is especially deftly handled, as is the symbolism of the two birds in the sky glimpsed through the open window, soaring and free.

In the magazine the illustrations are printed separately from the text on decent quality smooth paper stock and the impressions are generally even and
rich. 'The Bishop and the Knight' (July 1862; Periodical Illustrations 4:xi) is a 208
powerful example of the artist's 'antiquarian' style with an especially happy contrast of light and dark – the bishop is brightly lit in a way that suggests a purity of thought and a clarity of comprehension:

> The Bishop's face grew ashy pale;
> Awhile he paused in dumb surprise –
> Then spoke, aversion in his mien,
> And horror in his eyes:
> "Ah, never at my feet did bow
> A Christian stained as deep as thou,
> I may not, dare not, shrive thee now."

The way the sinner is suffused with darkness adds strength to the text, some might think a little too obviously, yet the result is a potent one. The handling is so confident and intense and clearly demonstrates how in an illustration such as this Millais advances 'beyond decoration'. One further point to make about the *Cornhill* is that within the body of the magazine the names of the artists are never mentioned, while those of the authors are occasionally given. It is tempt-

4 *The Outcast Mother*, p.616, dated 12 July 1839.

5 In 1861 Smith Elder published *Framley Parsonage* in three volumes containing the designs by Millais from the magazine. Michael Sadleir (1977, p.35) mentions 'In 1869 the novel was issued as a volume in Smith, Elder's series of Illustrated editions of Popular Works, bound in brown cloth and blocked in black and gold. In this form *Framley Parsonage* contains four of the original illustrations, and a picture title-page not previously published.' Exhaustive enquiries at libraries in the UK and US have failed to locate a copy of this book. It is entirely possible that Millais contributed this new title-page design, but without having seen it I can make no comment beyond this mention.

ing to read into this omission something about the status of illustration compared to text, but I think this suggestion should be treated with caution. After all, the illustrations are listed and are clearly of significance by their very presence, and Millais's recognisable monogram is almost invariably visible in the block.

Good Words, though in many ways a rival to the *Cornhill* in terms of readership, was an entirely different kind of periodical. Founded by Alexander Strahan (?1834–1918) in Edinburgh, it had an admittedly religious agenda, yet he himself was an unashamed populist. He was remarkable in that he saw illustration as of real importance in periodical publication, noting shrewdly, on looking back to the period before the launch of *Good Words*: 'Only in a most meagre and mean, or else in an utterly base, way did popular literature avail itself of the helps which I believed it could rightly obtain from Art for the purpose of adding to its own attractiveness and heightening its proper delights.'[6]

With such thoughts in mind Strahan produced in his magazine one of the most rewarding hunting grounds for fine illustration. While he never attracted the most vaunted literary names, the volume for 1862 contains some highly respected contributors. Mrs Craik (Dinah Mulock) appears with 'Mistress and Maid', and there are also to be found writings by Sarah Tytler (Henrietta Keddie), Mrs Gatty, Dora Greenwell, Horace Moule and Archbishop Whately. The major difference between the *Cornhill* and *Good Words* during this particular year is the far larger number of illustrations contained in the latter. Not merely the quantity but also the distinction of the artists is little short of staggering. As well as Millais there is a roll-call of almost all the most distinguished illustrators of the day: Holman Hunt, Burne-Jones, Frederick Sandys, Whistler, Simeon Solomon, Frederick Walker, Charles Keene, Arthur Boyd Houghton and several others. Millais's work for 'Mistress and Maid' is of the highest order, showing his innate understanding of women, their clothing, movement and gestures. A notable example is the group shown waiting anxious-
243 ly at the station (1862, p.225; Periodical Illustrations 5:vi). Here in so tiny a space an entire range of emotions and tensions is delicately outlined. The figures are clearly differentiated and the strength of the drawing comes through in feature and pose, despite the poor paper. The background of the busy station is also graphically suggested.

The following year saw Millais provide the first twelve designs for 'The Parables of Our Lord' in the same magazine, but it must be admitted that they make little impact here. The 'Parables' received far better printing treatment when they were reprinted with additions in book form in 1864 and it is in this guise that these outstanding drawings should be examined.

254 It was during 1864 that 'Polly', one of the artist's most popular and enduring illustrations, was published. It was reprinted again and again, appearing in innumerable children's books over many years, often cut down and in increasingly feeble impressions. Yet its cloying sentimentality makes it difficult for a contemporary reader to stomach, despite its facility and initial charm.

Once a Week came from the same publishing stable as *Punch*, Bradbury and Evans, and it bore the subtitle *An illustrated Miscellany of Literature, Art,*

6 Alexander Strahan, 'Twenty Years of a Publisher's Life' in *Day of Rest*, n.s. 3 (1881), p.15.

Science and Popular Information. It started publication on 2 July 1859 with Samuel Lucas (1818–1868) as editor and was intended as a direct competitor with Dickens's two magazines, *All the Year Round* and *Household Words*, neither of which was illustrated. While it had no specifically religious intent like *Good Words*, neither did it aim to ape the lofty intellectual tone embodied in the *Cornhill*: instead, it set out to inform, amuse and entertain its middle-class commuting readership with a refreshing lightness of touch.[7] Yet it also managed to attract some leading writers, including Harriet Martineau, Charles Reade, Tennyson, George Meredith and Shirley Brooks among a host of others.

In terms of illustration, Millais appears (at least in the first few months) somewhat unusually flanked by artists almost exclusively from a *Punch* background – most notably Hablot Knight Browne (Phiz), Charles Keene, John Leech and John Tenniel. However, within a very brief period, artists of the calibre of Matthew James Lawless, Holman Hunt, Frederick Walker, Whistler, Frederick Sandys and Edward Poynter were contributing, making *Once a Week* arguably the most contradictory and remarkable illustrated periodical of the period. Millais made more drawings for this organ than for any other, and among them are some examples of his very finest work. Several of his designs for poetry have already been examined (pp.14–17), but it is the drawings for Harriet Martineau's historical stories, some termed a trifle archly, 'Historiettes', which reveal Millais as a consummate illustrator. In 'Sister Anna's Probation', a tale set at the time of Henry VIII, for example, Millais produces a group of five
designs that are among his best. The opening drawing, 9:xxviii (15 March 1862, 280
p.309), is a case in point. Here the young Anna, sitting at her mother's feet, confides to her her thoughts on taking holy orders. The intensity on the face of the girl, her pose and her air of deep concentration are wonderfully captured by the artist with not a trace of over-prettiness or sentimentality. Similarly in later designs, both for this tale and for others by the same author, Millais demonstrates a remarkable intensity and depth of thought. Unfortunately the poor paper and mediocre printing prevent a full appreciation of many of these admirable works: the worst example is probably Millais's first contribution to
the magazine, 'Magenta', which appeared on 2 July 1859 (p.10; Periodical 263
Illustrations 9:i). Here the girl's face is all but obliterated by the wretched production and printing.

Nevertheless, *Once a Week* remains a magazine of the first importance for Millais. Here he could illustrate both prose and poetry and was able to venture into realms such as Breton verse translated by Tom Taylor, as well as historical and even mythical subjects. It gave him scope to explore his entire range of styles and skills, and hence is well worth the effort involved in tackling the mediocre printing and second-rate paper.

Saint Pauls started publication in October 1867 from the house of Virtue and Company, with Trollope as its editor. Here he serialised arguably one of his finest political novels, *Phineas Finn, the Irish Member*, and Millais was once again engaged to illustrate it. Despite Swain's careful engraving, the designs for

7 The completion of the rail network in the mid-1850s was a significant factor in terms of distribution of reading-matter to an increasingly mobile public. Virtually every station boasted a W. H. Smith bookstall and there is little doubt that numbers of weeklies such as *Once a Week* were routinely available to passengers.

this novel seem to me among Millais's weakest and least inspired. Even one of
316 the best, 'I wish you would be in earnest with me', is little more than formulaic
and disappointingly conventional – it feels for all the world as if Millais has
199 wearied of the task of drawing for Trollope. One has merely to return to his
to earlier work, especially for *Framley Parsonage*, to see an enormous difference in
206 application and sensitivity.

One or two of the remaining periodicals deserve note, especially *London Society*, *Churchman's Family Magazine* and *The Argosy*. While Millais made just a tiny number of designs for these, most are worth looking up. 'The Sighing
193 of the Shell' in *The Argosy* of June 1866 (Periodical Illustrations 1:i) exemplifies
many of the artist's virtues as an illustrator. Drawn almost like a miniature, it sets the lovers in an arbour-like frame and the atmosphere is one of supreme tenderness where Millais not merely evokes George MacDonald's verse but adds another dimension – he gives the reader a visual equivalent which immeasurably enhances and strengthens the written word:

> Listen, darling, and tell to me
> What the murmurer says to thee,
> Murmuring 'twixt a song and a moan,
> Changing neither tune nor tone.

As an illustrator of periodical literature, and especially in *Once a Week*, Millais reveals in telling ways crucial differences in treatment when compared with his achievement in books. Despite being so frequently pressed to meet deadlines, he rarely produces drawings of a workaday nature: in some instances the pressure seems to have impelled him to draw in his most appealing and vivacious style.

In particular, his designs for the stories of Harriet Martineau enabled him to deal with historical subjects that are not mere period pieces, but of such psychological depth as to encourage the reader to return and revalue these neglected tales. Similarly with the mythological texts, and especially in the verses translated from the Breton, Millais produces several designs of real nobility and power. Stylistically, too, there is a refreshing variety to be found, especially when comparing the 'scratchy' technique in *Once a Week* with the more detailed hatching present in the designs made for 'Mistress and Maid' in *Good Words*.

Thus the periodicals offer a rewarding perspective on Millais, and there are enough differences in approach and handling within this group to ensure that they should not be neglected in favour of the books. Millais is an essentially literary artist who by his draughtsmanship and his refined sensitivity to words is able to impart to the reader an enlarged appreciation of the text, whether it is to be found in books or in periodicals. It is this feature, perhaps above all, that marks him out as one of the most perceptive and profound illustrators of the nineteenth century.

APPENDIX ONE

Two Drawings on Wood

Few drawings by Millais on wood blocks remain in existence. However, three related to *The Parables of Our Lord* are known. That for 'The Marriage Feast' is in the Victoria and Albert Museum, while those for 'The Importunate Friend' and 'The Good Shepherd' are held in the Johannesburg Art Gallery. Most of the blocks on which Millais drew were cut by the engraver and, although retained for many years for the purpose of proofing, were eventually discarded. Hence the interest and significance of the two in a private collection published and reproduced here for the first time. Both reveal the artist working out ideas for designs that were eventually altered in the published image. These particular blocks were not engraved.

1. 'Tannhaüser', graphite on boxwood related to the design published in 276
Once a Week, 17 August 1861, page 211 (Periodical Illustrations 9:xxiii).
115 × 95 mm (4½ × 3¾ in), depth 23 mm (⅞ in).
Geoffroy Richard Everett Millais Collection.

248 2. 'Mistress and Maid', graphite on boxwood related to the design published in *Good Words*, September 1862, page 545 (Periodical Illustrations 5:xi).
152 × 114 mm (6 × 4½ in), depth 23 mm (⅞ in).
Geoffroy Richard Everett Millais Collection.

APPENDIX TWO

Millais and the Engravers

While this may not perhaps be the place to undertake a detailed analysis of the contact between Millais and his principal engravers such as the Dalziel Brothers and Joseph Swain it is, nevertheless, a relationship of genuine importance in terms of his illustrations. His method was first to produce rough preparatory drawings almost invariably in graphite and then go on to sketches of particular figures. When satisfied with his progress he would develop these into a finished design which would be very close to what would appear on the printed page. Ink was often employed for these designs which would be transferred onto a boxwood block in reverse, frequently with the aid of tracing paper. When Millais did this himself such sheets were usually destroyed in the cutting. However, by 1863 such drawings could be transferred to blocks photographically, and in consequence many more of them tended to survive than had done so in earlier years.

The blocks themselves were engraved by employees of chiefly London based concerns such as the Dalziel Brothers, Joseph Swain and others and it is a matter of regret that the individual names of these practitioners are so rarely recorded. Nevertheless, it is to be hoped that by examining the reproductions in the present study some notion of the remarkable skills and sensitivity of these largely forgotten people may be discerned. It is also worth challenging the long-held belief that the work of the various engraving shops cannot be differentiated. In the case of the two leading firms nothing could be further from the truth.

While the Dalziel Brothers might produce designs that, on occasion, appeared scratchy, summary and lightly printed, yet at the same time, when faced by Tennyson or the Parables their engravers discovered reserves of delicacy and minute gradations of tone which demand appreciation and admiration.

In contrast, however, the images emanating from the workshops of Joseph Swain possess a solidity and firmness of line which are both instantly recognisable and invariably highly satisfying optically. Many excellent examples of Swain's particular style of wood-engraving are to be found in the pages of *Once a Week* despite the poor quality of the paper used and the sometimes slipshod printing. These images are also often far darker in appearance when compared with those engraved by other businesses.

When the engraver had completed his or her (many of the engravers were women) initial engraving of the block a few proof impressions were taken and shown to Millais for him to check. He would then make numerous corrections and improvements both in graphite and in Chinese White to the proofs which were returned to the engraver so that the changes might be included on the block. When the artist was satisfied that his latest thoughts had been properly incorporated he would give his approval. Such blocks were generally used only for proofing, and metal electrotype facsimiles were used for printing in the books and, indeed, in many of the periodicals. This method, invented in 1839, could produce faithful reproductions of wood blocks in metal and these were vastly superior in quality to those obtained employing the previous system called 'stereotyping' in which duplicate blocks were created by means of a mould. Hence, should an electrotype ever become broken or damaged in any way it was a relatively simple process to produce a replacement using the original wood block as a master.

The Etchings

It appears that all the etchings, with the exception of number 31 (the roundel for *The Lineage and Pedigree of the Family of Millais)* are by the artist himself. While such a comment may appear overwhelmingly self-evident, it is, nevertheless, worth stating when examining a group of designs where so many are engraved after the artist's original drawings.

Millais excelled as an etcher and his first, the unpublished 'St. Agnes of Intercession', number 1 (1850), has claims to being his greatest. It is redolent of the first flush of Pre-Raphaelite intensity and, as a recent commentator has remarked, 'Millais created a pitiably expressive etching, the pain upon the sitter's face countered by the intense concentration of her artist lover as he stands before the easel, brush poised to record all that he sees.'[1] All the other etchings, numbering just eleven, and all published, are worth examining as each reveals a command and control of the needle which makes one regret that he produced so few.

The Steel Engravings

Millais was exceptionally well served by some of the finest steel-engravers at work during the period. Thomas Oldham Barlow (1824–1889) was responsible for 'When first I met thee' in Moore's *Irish Melodies* (1856) number 5, a print which reveals his complete mastery of line and tone, while John Saddler (1813–1892) produced most of the frontispieces in the unjustly neglected Hurst and Blackett *Standard Library* Series. While all of these repay study, perhaps the most distinguished, both in terms of Millais's design and as an example of Saddler's understated sensitivity, is number 24 'Cosette' for Hugo's *Les Misérables* [1864].

The term 'steel-engraving' is a misleading one. Because it is so difficult to hand engrave on to steel plates (introduced in the 1820s), they were, in the event, usually etched, and hence a steel-engraving can be said to be made up of almost entirely etched lines but set down in the manner akin to that found in copper engravings.[2]

1 Rodney Engen, *Pre-Raphaelite Prints*, London: Lund Humphries, 1995, p.30. The book contains a most useful critique of Millais as an etcher and a list of the large etchings, mezzotints and photogravures made after the oil paintings. The latter is an area not covered in the present work. In the list of etchings by Millais himself, one, entitled 'The Fisher Girl', is no longer considered to be the work of the artist.

2 For a detailed description of the technique see A. Griffiths, *Prints and Printmaking*, London: British Museum Press, 1996, p. 39.

THE BOOK ILLUSTRATIONS

1850

1. Etching, 'St. Agnes of Intercession'. 145 × 227 mm (5¾ × 9 in). Image 107 × 178 mm (4¼ × 7 in). [1850.]

Intended for the fifth number of *The Germ* but never published. It was to have accompanied a story by Dante Gabriel Rossetti, which he originally intended to illustrate himself, entitled 'St. Agnes of Intercession'. In the event he found himself dissatisfied with his own effort and, on seeing a proof of it on March 28th, 1850, deliberately damaged the surface of the plate ensuring that no further impressions could be taken from it. It seems that Millais began work on his plate shortly after this date. However, on May 23rd, 1850, it was decided to publish no further issues of *The Germ*. There is an impression in the City Museum and Art Gallery, Birmingham (1906 P625 (2)), and another in the Victoria and Albert Museum given in 1910 by Sir Frank Short (E 5150/1910). A further impression is in the Yale Center for British Art, New Haven.

1852

2. W. Wilkie Collins, ***Mr. Wray's Cash-Box;*** *or, The Mask and the Mystery. A Christmas Sketch*. Richard Bentley, 1852. [12622.b.13]

1st edition. Frontispiece etching entitled 'Mr Wray's Cash-Box' with 'London, Richard Bentley, 1852' below and signed 'J. E. Millais' in the plate. Image 114 × 72 mm (4½ × 2⅞ in).

Geoffroy Millais has drawn my attention to the existence of a variant of this plate. It was shown in an exhibition at the Shepherd Gallery, New York, 'Pre-Raphaelite and Academic Drawings, Watercolours, Paintings and Sculpture', 27 April–9 June 1983, no. 64. This impression is lettered 'The New Neckcloth' and is signed in the plate as above. The only tentative explanation I can offer is that this might have been intended for an American edition, since although 'Neckcloth' does appear on occasion in English literature it is seen infrequently. If such an edition was published, I have failed to trace it.

1855

3. William Allingham, ***The Music Master,*** *A Love Song, and two series of Day and Night Songs*. George Routledge and Co., 1855. [C.58. b.21]

Wood-engraving by Dalziel after Millais entitled 'The Fireside Story' facing page 216. 76 × 125 mm (3 × 4⅞ in). The poem is entitled *Frost in the Holidays.*

The book also contains seven designs by Arthur Hughes and one by Dante Gabriel Rossetti. It is an enlarged and illustrated edition of *Day and Night Songs*, also published by Routledge the previous year. There was a second edition in 1860 published by Bell and Daldy and an unillustrated reprint in 1884. The Rossetti drawing is the celebrated 'Maids of Elfen-mere'.

Allingham wrote in the preface (p.ix): 'Those excellent painters who on my behalf have submitted their genius to the risks of wood-engraving will, I hope, pardon me for placing a word of sincere thanks in the book they have honoured with this evidence, through art, of their valued friendship'.

1855 or 1856

4. **Reverend John Anderson, *The Pleasures of Home:*** *A Poem in Two Parts*. Arthur Hall, Virtue and Co., n.d. [1855/6]. [11649.d.36]

Frontispiece wood-engraved by Thomas Williams after Millais. 114 × 82 mm (4½ × 3¼ in).

The book is undated and the late Dr W. E. Fredeman believed 1855 to be the date of publication. However, the British Library copy bears a receipt date of 2 June 1856, hence I suggest the later year as likely to be correct. *The English Catalogue of Books* gives A. Hall, 1856.

1856

5. **Thomas Moore, *Irish Melodies*.** Longmans, Brown, Green and Longmans, 1856. [C.30.h.6]

Steel-engraving by T. O. Barlow after Millais entitled 'When first I met thee' facing page 84. 145 × 105 mm (5¾ × 4⅛ in). The original drawing was made in 1853, and first served as one of a group of drawings 'from modern life'.

1857

6. **Alfred Tennyson, *Poems*.** Edward Moxon, 1857 ('The Moxon Tennyson'). [11647.e.59]

Eighteen wood-engraved designs after Millais:

(i) Page 7. To *Mariana*. Engraved by Dalziel. 95 × 78 mm (3¾ × 3⅛ in).

(ii) Page 86. To *The Miller's Daughter*. Engraved by John Thompson. 92 × 83 mm (3⅝ × 3¼ in).

(iii) Page 93. To *The Miller's Daughter*. Engraved by John Thompson. 95 × 82 mm (3¾ × 3¼ in).

(iv) Page 109. To *The Sisters*. Engraved by Dalziel. 94 × 74 mm (3¾ × 2⅞ in).

(v) Page 149. To *A Dream of Fair Women* (Cleopatra). Engraved by William James Linton. 97 × 83 mm (3⅞ × 3¼ in).

(vi) Page 161. To *A Dream of Fair Women* (Queen Eleanor). Engraved by Dalziel. 83 × 96 mm (3¼ × 3⅞ in).

(vii) Page 172. To *The Death of the Old Year*. Engraved by Dalziel. 97 × 83 mm (3⅞ × 3¼ in).

(viii) Page 213. To *Dora*. Engraved by Thomas Williams. 93 × 80 mm (3⅝ × 3⅛ in).

(ix) Page 219. To *Dora*. Engraved by John Thompson. 87 × 80 mm (3⅜ × 3⅛ in).

(x) Page 242. To *The Talking Oak*. Engraved by John Thompson. 82 × 98 mm (3¼ × 3⅞ in).

(xi) Page 255. To *The Talking Oak*. Engraved by Dalziel. 95 × 83 mm (3¾ × 3¼ in).

(xii) Page 267. To *Locksley Hall*. Engraved by John Thompson. 94 × 80 mm (3¾ × 3⅛ in).

(xiii) Page 274. To *Locksley Hall*. Engraved by Dalziel. 95 × 80 mm (3¾ × 3⅛ in).

(xiv) Page 309. To *St. Agnes' Eve*. Engraved by Dalziel. 98 × 73 mm (3⅞ × 2⅞ in).

(xv) Page 317. To *The Day-Dream*. Engraved by William James Linton. 82 × 97 mm (3¼ × 3⅞ in).

(xvi) Page 323. To *The Day-Dream*. Engraved by Charles Thurston Thompson. 83 × 95 mm (3¼ × 3¾ in).

(xvii) Page 340. To *Edward Gray*. Engraved by John Thompson. 85 × 83 mm (3⅜ × 3¼ in).

(xviii) Page 353. To *The Lord of Burleigh*. Engraved by Dalziel. 83 × 96 mm (3¼ × 3¾ in).

7. **Reverend Robert Aris Willmott (ed.), *The Poets of the Nineteenth Century*.** George Routledge and Co., 1857. [1347.I.10]

(i) Page 123. To *The Dream* (Byron). Engraved by Dalziel. 124 × 93 mm (4⅞ × 3⅝ in).

(ii) Page 137. To *Love* (Coleridge). Engraved by Dalziel. 126 × 94 mm (5 × 3¾ in).

8. ***Etchings for the Art Union of London by the Etching Club***. 1857. [BM 190* a.17.1865-1-14-951]

Etching, 'The Young Mother'. 205 × 160 mm (8⅛ × 6¼ in). Image 140 × 144 5½ × 5⅝ in).

Signed in the plate in monogram and 'J. E. Millais A.R.A.' and numbered '29'. On laid India paper. In the state before letters in the Victoria and Albert Museum the print (V&A 247) is dated 1856.

Geoffroy Millais makes the following suggestions about the identitities of the subjects. Millais's first child, a son, Everett, was born at Annat Lodge, Perth on 30 May 1856. If, as seems likely, the etching was made later the same year in Scotland then it is probable that the scene depicts the artist's wife, Effie (1828–97) cradling Everett (d.1897) against a Scottish landscape.

1858

9. ***Lays of the Holy Land from Ancient and Modern Poets***. James Nisbet and Co., 1858. [1347.h.10]

Page 51. To *Moses on the Nile* (James Grahame): 'The Finding of Moses'. Wood-engraved by Dalziel. 139 × 101 mm (5½ × 4 in).

There were later, undated reissues of this book, as well as a dated second edition in 1871.

10. ***Passages from the Poems of Thomas Hood, Illustrated by the Junior Etching Club***. Ernest Gambart, 1858. [BM 190* b.16.1863-4-11-176, 1863-4-11-193]

Two etchings:

(i) Plate 10. 'The Bridge of Sighs'. 178 × 125 mm (7 × 4⅞ in). Image 118 × 93 mm (4⅝ × 3⅝ in).

On Chine appliqué. Signed in the plate in monogram.

(ii) Plate 27. 'Ruth'. 178 x 125 mm (7 x 4⅞ in). Image 129 x 88 mm (5⅛ x 3½ in). On Chine appliqué. Signed and dated 1858 in the plate.

11. Charles Mackay (ed.), *The Home Affections Pourtrayed by the Poets.* George Routledge and Co., 1858. [1347.h.12]

Two wood-engravings after Millais:

(i) Page 245. To *There's Nae Luck about the House* (William Julius Mickle). Engraved by Dalziel. 123 x 93 mm (4⅞ x 3⅝ in).

(ii) Page 359. To *The Border Widow* (anonymous ballad). Engraved by Dalziel. 94 x 126 mm (3¾ x 5 in).

1861

12. Dinah Mulock (Mrs Craik), *John Halifax, Gentleman.* Hurst and Blackett *Standard Library*, volume ii [1861]. [1608.505]

Steel-engraved frontispiece by John Saddler after Millais. Dated 1861 in the plate. 132 x 84 mm (5¼ x 3¼ in).

13. Dinah Mulock (Mrs Craik), *Nothing New.* Hurst and Blackett *Standard Library*, volume xvii [1861]. [12618.d.17]

Steel-engraved frontispiece by John Saddler after Millais. Dated 1861 in the plate. 134 x 84 mm (5¼ x 3¼ in).

14. [Julia Cecilia Stretton], *The Valley of a Hundred Fires.* Hurst and Blackett *Standard Library*, volume xix [1861]. [12618.f.24]

Steel-engraved frontispiece by John Saddler after Millais. Dated 1861 in the plate. 133 x 84 mm (5¼ x 3¼ in).

1861/2

15. *Passages from Modern English Poets Illustrated by the Junior Etching Club.* Day and Son [1861/2]. [1751.b.19] [BM 190*a.18.1863-2-14-1366]

Etching, *Indolence* (anonymous). Signed in the plate in monogram and dated 1861. Also with 'J. E. Millias' [*sic*] (lower right) and 'Pl 10' (top right); below, 'London. Published December 1st 1861, by Day and Son, Lith to the Queen.' 175 x 253 mm (6⅞ x 10 in). Image 91 x 154 mm (3⅝ x 6⅛ in).

For this illustration Alaric A. Watts chose 'Indolence', anonymous, and 'Love in Idleness' by Laman Blanchard, and 'Summer Idleness' by Jeremiah Holmes Wiffen as poems that 'seemed calculated to illustrate the predominant sentiment of the design'. An inscription in pencil on an early proof (Private Collection) identifies the child as L. J. Barlow.

The dating of the book is complex, with a preface dated 1862 but plates dated 1861. See the present author's *Victorian Illustration* (London: Lund Humphries, 2004, pp.326–7) for a detailed bibliographical description. The figure is derived from Millais's painting *Spring (Apple Blossoms)* of 1856–9 and has been identified as Alice Elizabeth Gray (1845–1929), who was a younger sister of Millais's wife, Euphemia (Effie) Gray. (See *The Pre-Raphaelites*, exh. cat., London: Tate Gallery 1984 pp.171–3.)

16. Anthony Trollope, *Orley Farm*. Chapman and Hall, 1862. [C.190.e.15]

Two volumes with 40 wood-engraved illustrations by Dalziel after Millais. Originally issued in parts.

Volume 1:

(i) Frontispiece. 'Orley Farm'. 162 × 107 mm (6⅜ × 4¼ in).

(ii) Facing page 16. 'Sir Peregrine and his heir'. 159 × 105 mm (6¼ × 4⅛ in).

(iii) Facing page 37. 'There was sorrow in her heart, and deep thought in her mind'. 165 × 107 mm (6½ × 4¼ in).

(iv) Facing page 46. 'There is nothing like iron, Sir; nothing'. 167 × 105 mm (6⅝ × 4⅛ in).

(v) Facing page 73. 'And then they all marched out of the room, each with his own glass'. 167 × 105 mm (6⅝ × 4⅛ in).

(vi) Facing page 86. 'Mr. Furnival's welcome home'. 166 × 106 mm (6½ × 4⅛ in).

(vii) Facing page 98. 'Your son Lucius did say – shopping'. 168 × 106 mm (6⅝ × 4⅛ in).

(viii) Facing page 111. 'Over their wine'. 168 × 106 mm (6⅝ × 4⅛ in).

(ix) Facing page 136. 'Von Bauhr's Dream'. 166 × 108 mm (6½ × 4¼ in).

(x) Facing page 140. 'The English Von Bauhr and his pupil'. 168 × 107 mm (6⅝ × 4¼ in).

(xi) Facing page 169. 'Christmas at Noningsby. – Morning'. 167 × 107 mm (6⅝ × 4¼ in).

(xii) Facing page 175. 'Christmas at Noningsby. – Evening'. 167 × 105 mm (6⅝ × 4⅛ in).

(xiii) Facing page 201. 'Why should I not?' 169 × 107 mm (6⅝ × 4¼ in).

(xiv) Facing page 216. 'Monkton Grange'. 171 × 106 mm (6¾ × 4⅛ in).

(xv) Facing page 226. 'Felix Graham in Trouble'. 169 × 106 mm (6⅝ × 4⅛ in).

(xvi) Facing page 241. 'Footsteps in the corridor'. 168 × 106 mm (6⅝ × 4⅛ in).

(xvii) Facing page 257. 'The Angel of Light'. 173 × 109 mm (6¾ × 4¼ in).

(xviii) Facing page 283. 'Lucius Mason in his study'. 167 × 107 mm (6⅝ × 4¼ in).

(xix) Facing page 289. 'Peregrine's Eloquence'. 168 × 107 mm (6⅝ × 4¼ in).

(xx) Facing page 306. 'Lady Staveley interrupting her son and Sophia Furnival'. 167 × 106 mm (6⅝ × 4⅛ in).

Volume 2:

(xxi) Frontispiece. 'Lady Mason leaving the court'. 170 × 106 mm (6¾ × 4⅛ in).

(xxii) Facing page 11. 'John Kenneby and Miriam Dockwrath'. 168 × 106 mm (6⅝ × 4⅛ in).

(xxiii) Facing page 30 or sometimes page 32. 'Guilty'. 168 × 106 mm (6⅝ × 4⅛ in).

(xxiv) Facing page 40 or 41. 'Lady Mason after her Confession'. 168 × 107 mm (6⅝ × 4¼ in).

(xxv) Facing page 48. 'Bread Sauce is so ticklish'. 168 × 107 mm (6⅝ × 4¼ in).

(xxvi) Facing page 77. 'Never is a very long word'. 171 × 108 mm (6¾ × 4¼ in).

(xxvii) Facing page 89.'"Tom" she said, "I have come back"'. 172 × 108 mm (6¾ × 4¼ in).

(xxviii) Facing page 97. 'Lady Mason going before the Magistrates'. 172 × 108 mm (6¾ × 4¼ in).

(xxix) Facing page 126. 'Sir Peregrine at Mr. Round's Office'. 172 × 108 mm (6¾ × 4¼ in).

(xxx) Facing page 145. 'Tell me, Madelaine, are you happy now?' 169 × 107 mm (6⅝ × 4¼ in).

(xxxi) Facing page 148. 'No surrender'. 172 × 110 mm (6¾ × 4⅜ in).

(xxxii) Facing page 172 or 173. 'Mr. Chaffanbrass and Mr. Solomon Aram'. 171 × 107 mm (6¾ × 4¼ in).

(xxxiii) Facing page 190 or 191. 'The Court'. 171 × 105 mm (6¾ × 4⅛ in).

(xxxiv) Facing page 202 or 203. 'The Drawing-room at Noningsby'. 171 × 106 mm (6¾ × 4⅛ in).

(xxxv) Facing page 206. 'And how are they all at Noningsby?' 171 × 106 mm (6¾ × 4⅛ in).

(xxxvi) Facing page 240. 'How can I bear it?' 172 × 106 mm (6¾ × 4⅛ in).

(xxxvii) Facing page 247. 'Bridget Bolster in Court'. 170 × 107 mm (6¾ × 4¼ in).

(xxxviii) Facing page 264. 'Lucius Mason, as he leaned on the gate that was no longer his own'. 173 × 106 mm (6¾ × 4⅛ in).

(xxxix) Facing page 305. 'Farewell!' 171 × 106 mm (6¾ × 4⅛ in).

(xl) Facing page 314. 'Farewell'. 171 × 105 mm (6¾ × 4⅛ in).

17. Dinah Mulock (Mrs Craik), *Mistress and Maid.* Hurst and Blackett *Standard Library*, volume xxvi [1862]. [12618.d.16]

Steel-engraved frontispiece by John Saddler after Millais. 129 × 86 mm (4⅛ × 3⅜ in).

1863

18. Anne Isabella Robertson, *Myself and my Relatives.* Sampson Low, 1863. [12631.cc.12]

Steel-engraved frontispiece by Henry Adlard after Millais. 136 × 80 mm (5⅜ × 3⅛ in).

Signed in the plate in monogram lower left and dated 1862. Entitled 'Myself and my Relatives', it relates to a scene described on page 185.

I am indebted to Maroussia Oakley for having discovered this book and having alerted me to its existence.

19. **Sarah Tytler (Henrietta Keddie),** ***Papers for Thoughtful Girls.*** Alexander Strahan and Co., 1863. [12632.cc.31]

Four wood-engravings after Millais:

(i) Frontispiece. 'Cis Berry's Arrival'. Engraved by Dalziel. 139 × 85 mm (5½ × 3⅜ in).

Relates to a scene in the chapter entitled 'Favour' on page 109.

(ii) Facing page 10. 'Our Sister Grizel' to 'Youth'. Engraved by Dalziel. 139 × 88mm (5½ × 3½ in).

(iii) Facing page 190. 'Dame Dorothy' to 'Friendship'. Engraved by Dalziel. 139 × 87 mm (5½ × 3½ in).

(iv) Facing page 268 to 'Kindliness', the section called 'Nürnberg Eggs'. The design is entitled 'Herr Willy Koenig'. Engraved by Dalziel. 138 × 87 mm (5⅜ × 3⅜ in).

20. ***Wordsworth's Poems for the Young.*** Alexander Strahan and Co., 1863. [11611.bbb.34 (1866 edn)]

Title-page vignette of a little girl reading intently. Engraved by Dalziel after Millais. 50 × 37 mm (2 × 1½ in).

1864

21. ***The Cornhill Gallery.*** Smith Elder and Co., 1864. [1753.b]

Twenty-nine wood-engravings after Millais, all taken from *The Cornhill Magazine*. For details see Periodical Illustrations 4.

22. **Matthew Browne (William Brighty Rands),** ***Lilliput Levée.*** Alexander Strahan and Co., 1864. [11650.e.15]

Three wood-engravings after Millais, all reprints:

(i) Title-page vignette reprinted from *Wordsworth's Poems for the Young* (see no.20 above).

(ii) Facing page 79. 'Prince Philibert' reprinted from *Good Words* (1864). See Periodical Illustrations 5:xx.

(iii) Facing page 91. 'Polly' reprinted from *Good Words* (1864). See Periodical Illustrations 5:xviii.

23. **W. Wilkie Collins,** ***No Name.*** Sampson Low, Son and Marston. Cheap Edition. 1864. [12654.c.13]

Steel-engraved frontispiece by John Saddler after Millais. 109 × 81 mm (4¼ × 3¼ in).

Entitled 'No Name – One half-hour', it is signed in monogram and dated 1863 in the plate. Additionally dated below 'Novr 23 1863'. Relates to a scene on page 368.

The book was published on 1 December 1863, but is dated 1864 on the title-page.

24. Victor Hugo, *Les Misérables.* Hurst and Blackett *Standard Library*, volume xxviii [1864]. [012550.cc.19]

Steel-engraved frontispiece by John Saddler after Millais. 128 × 84 mm (5 × 3¼ in).

Entitled 'Cosette', it is dated 1863 in the plate. Additionally dated below 'Feb 12th 1864'. Early impressions bear 'J.E. Millais A.R.A.' at foot of plate, while later ones have 'Sir J.E. Millais R.A.'. The book was much reissued. Relates to a scene on page 319.

25. J.E. Millais, *The Parables of Our Lord and Saviour Jesus Christ.* Routledge, Warne and Routledge, 1864. [3226.f.24]

An undated reprint was published in 1885 by the Society for Promoting Christian Knowledge.

Twenty wood-engravings by Dalziel after Millais. Twelve of these designs originally appeared in *Good Words* for 1863. These were 'The Parable of the Leaven', 'The Parable of the Virgins', 'The Prodigal Son', 'The Good Samaritan', 'The Unjust Judge', 'The Pharisee and the Publican', 'The Hid Treasure', 'The Pearl of Great Price', 'The Lost Piece of Silver', 'The Parable of the Sower', 'The Unmerciful Servant' and 'The Labourers in the Vineyard'. See Periodical Illustrations 5.

(i) 'The Sower'. 140 × 108 mm (5½ × 4¼ in).

(ii) 'The Leaven'. 140 × 108 mm (5½ × 4¼ in).

(iii) 'The Tares'. 140 × 108 mm (5½ × 4¼ in).

(iv) 'The Hidden Treasure'. 140 × 108 mm (5½ × 4¼ in).

(v) 'The Pearl of Great Price'. 140 × 108 mm (5½ × 4¼ in).

(vi) 'The Unmerciful Servant'. 140 × 108 mm (5½ × 4¼ in).

(vii) 'The Labourers in the Vineyard'. 139 × 108 mm (5½ × 4¼ in).

(viii) 'The Wicked Husbandmen'. 140 × 108 mm (5½ × 4¼ in).

(ix) 'The Wise and Foolish Virgins'. 140 × 108 mm (5½ × 4¼ in).

(x) 'The Foolish Virgins'. 140 × 108 mm (5½ × 4¼ in).

(xi) 'The Good Samaritan'. 139 × 108 mm (5½ × 4¼ in).

(xii) 'The Importunate Friend'. 138 × 108 mm (5½ × 4¼ in).

(xiii) 'The Marriage Feast'. 140 × 108 mm (5½ × 4¼ in).

(xiv) 'The Lost Sheep'. 140 × 107 mm (5½ × 4¼ in).

(xv) 'The Lost Piece of Silver'. 140 × 108 mm (5½ × 4¼ in).

(xvi) 'The Prodigal Son'. 139 × 108 mm (5½ × 4¼ in).

(xvii) 'The Rich Man and Lazarus'. 139 × 108 mm (5½ × 4¼ in).

(xviii) 'The Unjust Judge'. 140 × 108 mm (5½ × 4¼ in).

(xix) 'The Pharisee and the Publican'. 140 × 108 mm (5½ × 4¼ in).

(xx) 'The Good Shepherd'. 140 × 108 mm (5½ × 4¼ in).

26. **Caroline Elizabeth Sarah Norton** (later **Stirling-Maxwell**), ***Lost and Saved.*** Hurst and Blackett *Standard Library*, volume xxvii [1864]. [12618.d.25]

Steel-engraved frontispiece by John Saddler after Millais. 128 × 84 mm (5 × 3¼ in).

Entitled 'Lost and Saved', signed in the plate and dated beneath '15th December 1863' with 'J.E. Millais A.R.A' to the left and 'John Saddler' to the right. Relates to a scene in Chapter 43 on page 242.

27. **Anthony Trollope, *Rachel Ray.*** Chapman and Hall, Standard Editions of Popular Authors series, 1864. [Private Collection]

Steel-engraved frontispiece by an unidentified engraver after Millais. 122 × 81 mm (4¾ × 3¼ in).

28. **Anthony Trollope, *The Small House at Allington.*** Smith Elder and Co., 2 volumes, 1864. [12623.f.56]

For the illustrations see Periodical Illustrations 4:xii–xxx. The design on the title-page of the book edition appears uniquely here:

(i) 'The Croquet Match'. 140 × 88 mm (5½ × 3½ in).

Engraved by Swain after Millais. Title and author's name. The title above and 'BY' on the chimney and 'Anthony Trollope' on the façade above the window of the house. With 'Smith Elder and Co' on the back of the bench with '65, Cornhill' and '1864' below.

The only design engraved by Swain for this book. The other blocks exhibit a marked deterioration of impression when compared with those in the periodical issue.

1865

29. ***Dalziel's Illustrated Arabian Nights Entertainments.*** Ward, Lock and Tyler, 1865 [originally published in monthly parts between January 1864 and September 1865]. [12410.h.8]

Two wood-engravings by Dalziel after Millais:

(i) Page 97. 'Zobeidè discovers the young man reading the Koran', from 'The History of Zobeidè'. March 1864. 170 × 128 mm (6⅝ × 5 in).

The scene depicted is described on page 98.

(ii) Page 105. 'Aminè and the Lady', from 'The History of Aminè'. March 1864. 167 × 124 mm (6⅝ × 4⅞ in).

The scene depicted is described on page 103.

30. **Tom Taylor (ed. and trans.), *Ballads and Songs of Brittany.*** Macmillan and Co., 1865. [2288.d.15]

Four wood-engravings reprinted from *Once a Week*. For details see Periodical Illustrations 9:xxxvi, v, xxxiv, xxvi.

(i) Facing page 34. 'The Drowning of Kaer-Is'.

(ii) Facing page 65. 'The Plague of Elliant'.

(iii) Facing page 75. 'The Crusader's Wife'.

(iv) Facing page 129. 'The Battle of the Thirty'.

31. **J. Bertrand Payne, *The Lineage and Pedigree of the Family of Millais.*** London, privately printed, 1865. [9903.l.2]

Frontispiece etching roundel showing the family coat of arms including shield, helmet, etc. On India paper appliqué signed below in facsimile 'John Everett Millais' and 'By whom this Plate was Designed, Etched & Presented to the Work'. Diameter 68 mm (2⅝ in).

I am grateful to Rupert Maas and Malcolm Warner for having alerted me to the existence of a letter from Millais to Payne of 12 July 1862 (private collection), saying that he could not find time to do the etching himself and 'so I got it done by a good man artistically' (personal correspondence, April 2003).

32. **Henry Leslie, *Little Songs for Me to Sing.*** Cassell, Petter and Galpin, 1865. [11648.bb.53]

Seven wood-engravings by Joseph Swain after Millais:

(i) Untitled frontispiece. 100 × 100 mm (4 × 4 in).

(ii) 'Twinkle, Twinkle, Little Star'. 100 × 100 mm (4 × 4 in).

(iii) 'Little Brother Charlie'. 96 × 98 mm (3¾ × 3⅞ in).

(iv) 'God's Works'. 100 × 100 mm (4 × 4 in).

(v) 'Mary's Little Lamb'. 100 × 100 mm (4 × 4 in).

(vi) 'The Sweet Story of Old'. 98 × 98 mm (3⅞ × 3⅞ in).

(vii) 'Morning and Evening Hymns'. 99 × 102 mm (3⅞ × 4 in).

33. ***A Selection of Etchings by the Etching Club.*** Joseph Cundall, 1865. [BM 190* b.15.1866-12-8-139]

Etching, 'Happy Springtime', on laid India paper. Signed in monogram and dated 1860 in the plate. 243 × 163 mm (9⅝ × 6⅜ in). Image 134 × 100 mm (5¼ × 4 in).

Geoffroy Millais suggests that the print may show the artist's wife, Effie, holding their eldest daughter, Effie Gray Millais (1858–1911).

34. **Frederick Locker, *A Selection from the Work of Frederick Locker.*** Edward Moxon and Co., Moxon's Miniature Poets series, 1865. [11602.bbb.34]

Frontispiece etched portrait of Locker. Signed in monogram. Image 68 × 57 mm (2⅝ × 2¼ in). The book is illustrated by Richard Doyle; there is no mention of Millais.

35. **Eliza Tabor (Stephenson), *St. Olave's.*** Hurst and Blackett *Standard Library*, volume xxi. [1865]. [12618 d.19]

Steel-engraved frontispiece by John Saddler after Millais, 'Alice'. Signed in the plate in monogram and dated 16 October 1865. 131 × 83 mm (5⅛ × 3¼ in).

1866

36. **Daniel Defoe, *Robinson Crusoe*** (ed. J. W. Clark). Macmillan and Co. Golden Treasury Series, 1866. [12611.c.12]
Steel-engraved title-page design by an unidentified engraver after Millais. Signed in monogram and dated 1862 in the plate. 78 × 68 mm (3⅛ × 2⅝ in).

37. **[Jean Ingelow],** ***Studies for Stories from Girls' Lives.*** Alexander Strahan, 1866. [BM – de Beaumont Collection 1992-4-6-141]

Two wood-engravings by Swain after Millais:

(i) Frontispiece to 'The Cumberers', page 49. 137 × 87 mm (5⅜ × 3⅜ in).

(ii) Facing page 309 to 'The Stolen Treasure'. 137 × 88 mm (5⅜ × 3½ in).

38. ***Millais's Collected Illustrations.*** Alexander Strahan, 1866. [1756.a.29]

Eighty-one wood-engravings by Swain and Dalziel after Millais. All the illustrations are reprints, with the exception of the title-page design. The two listed as 'unpublished', entitled here 'Watching' (61) and 'Pick-a-Pack' (79) appear *in Studies for Stories* (see above). However, according to *The English Catalogue of Books* this book actually appeared in December 1865, although dated 1866 on the title-page, while *Studies for Stories* was published in June 1866. Hence 'unpublished' here is technically correct.

Title-page design dated 1865 in the block engraved by Joseph Swain. 189 × 138 mm (7½ × 5⅜ in).

39. ***Pictures of Society Grave and Gay.*** Sampson, Low, Son and Marston, 1866. [11651.I.12]

Three wood-engravings by Dalziel and Joseph Swain after Millais.

(i) Facing page 26. 'I remember', reprint of 'Ah me! She was a winsome maid' from *London Society*, August 1862 (see Periodical Illustrations 8:i).

(ii) Facing page 178. 'A Moment of Suspense', reprint of '"Yes, Lewis," she said; "Quite satisfied"' from *London Society*, Christmas 1862 (see Periodical Illustrations 8:ii).

(iii) Facing page 192. 'A Matter of Moment', reprint of '"You will forgive me, won't you?" said Ralph' from *Churchman's Family Magazine*, February 1863 (see Periodical Illustrations 3:ii).

1867

40. ***Touches of Nature.*** Alexander Strahan, 1867. [1754.b.5]

Four wood-engravings by Dalziel after Millais.

These designs are taken from *Good Words*: see Periodical Illustrations 5. Two are from *The Parables of Our Lord*, published in the periodical in 1863, and the remaining two from *Mistress and Maid*, published the previous year. Confusingly, the designs are recaptioned. No.51, here called 'A Contrast', is in truth 'The Pharisee and the Publican'; no.66, here called 'The Lost Piece of Money', is 'The Lost Piece of Silver'.

41. **Charles Mackay (ed.),** ***A Thousand and One Gems of Poetry.*** George Routledge and Co., 1867. [11601.g.9]

Facing page 501 is a reprint of 'Edward Gray' from the edition of Tennyson's *Poems* (1857): see no.6 above.

42. ***Twenty-Nine Illustrations by John Everett Millais designed for the Cornhill Magazine.*** Smith Elder and Co., 1867. [D-1753.b.26 – MIC.A.10814 (1)]

Proof wood-engravings reprinted from the magazine. An illustrated Gift Book.

1868

43. **Johann Wolfgang von Goethe, *Egmont*.** Chapman and Hall, 1868. Translated by Arthur Duke Coleridge. [11745.e.33]

Frontispiece engraved by Swain after Millais. 94 × 138 mm (3¾ × 5⅜ in).

Refers to a scene on page 112.

1869

44. **H. Cholmondeley Pennell, *Puck on Pegasus*.** John Camden Hotten, 1869. [11651.e.10]

Facing page 140, engraved by Swain after Millais. 92 × 126 mm (3⅝ × 5 in).

This frankly curious design, here attributed to Millais, does not appear in the first edition of 1861 or in any later edition prior to that of 1869.

45. **Anthony Trollope, *Phineas Finn, The Irish Member*.** Virtue and Co., 1869. [12620.f.30]

Twenty wood-engravings first published in *Saint Pauls*. For details see Periodical Illustrations 12:i–xx.

1871

46. **Henry Leslie, *Henry Leslie's Musical Annual*.** Cassell, Petter and Galpin, 1871. [BL Music Library G.438]

Frontispiece steel-engraving by C.H. Jeens after Millais. Signed in monogram in the plate. 180 × 156 mm (7⅛ × 6⅛ in).

Entitled 'A Reverie' but referred to in the contents list as 'Girl at the Window', this was intended as a design for a group of songs by Tennyson set to music by Arthur Sullivan entitled 'The Window, or The Songs of the Wrens'. This particular image was to have accompanied a poem (the second in the set of 12) entitled 'At the Window' which opens 'Vine, Vine and Eglantine'. The song cycle was published in 1871 by Strahan and Co. without illustrations; the engraving was reissued in *The Magazine of Art* in September 1896. The original drawing was shown in the Millais exhibition of 1967 (no. 383 pp.95–6; see Select Bibliography) and is dated 1868.

A modern reprint of the song cycle by Raymond J. Walker (Wilmslow, 2002) contains a useful introduction relating the problematic road to publication and Tennyson's misgivings over the quality of his text. My thanks are due to John Allitt for kindly drawing my attention to this publication.

1872

47. **Matthew Browne (William Brighty Rands), *Lilliput Legends*.** Strahan and Co., 1872. [12808.m.17]

Reprint of the title-page vignette from *Wordsworth's Poems for the Young* (1863). See no.20 above.

48. ***Little Lily's Picture Book*.** George Routledge and Sons [1872]. [12807.f.75]

Facing page 72, a reprint of 'There's nae luck about the house' from *The Home Affections Pourtrayed by the Poets* (1858). See no.11 above.

49. *Etchings for the Art Union of London by the Etching Club.* 1872. [V&A E.3745-1902, E.3746-1902]

(i) 'Going to the Park'. Signed in monogram and 'J.E. Millais R.A.' lower left and title and numbered '2' in the plate. 186 × 134 mm (7⅜ × 5¼ in). Image 165 × 124 mm (6½ × 4⅞ in).

(ii) 'The Baby House'. Signed in monogram and 'J.E. Millais R.A.' lower left and title and numbered '9' in the plate. 143 × 184 mm (5⅝ × 7¼ in). Image 136 × 178 mm (5⅜ × 7 in).

Geoffroy Millais is confident that the etchings depict the artist's third and fourth daughters, Alice Sophia Caroline Millais (1862–1936) and Sophia Margaret Jameson Millais (1868–1907). He also points out that in 1872 the Millais family home was at 7 Cromwell Place, South Kensington, only a short distance from the park.

1873

50. **Francis Cowley Burnand,** ***Mokeanna! A Treble Temptation.*** Bradbury, Agnew and Co., 1873. [12331.aaaa.49]

Between pages 24 and 25. 'It is the Chapeau Blanc, The White Witness'. No engraver's name but probably by Joseph Swain. First published in *Punch* in 1863. See Periodical Illustrations 10. 112 × 168 mm (4⅜ × 6⅝ in).

51. ***Dawn to Daylight.*** Frederick Warne and Co. [1874]. [11165 1.i.22]

Page 65 is a reprint of 'Love' from *Poets of the Nineteenth Century* (1857), see 7:ii above. Here it accompanies lines from a poem by Michael Drayton:

'Since there's no help, come, let us kiss and part!'

1875

52. **Samuel Carter Hall,** ***An Old Story: A Temperance Tale.*** Virtue, Spalding and Co [1875]. [8435.b.48]

Frontispiece engraved by James Davis Cooper after Millais. 143 × 94 mm (5⅝ × 3¾ in).

Although no particular text is illustrated, the image is clearly of a woman waiting sorrowfully and anxiously for the return of her alcoholic husband.

1877

53. **Henry Frith,** ***Routledge's Holiday Album for Boys.*** George Routledge and Sons, 1877. [12809.bb.16]

Page 20 is a reprint of 'Swing Song' from *Once a Week*, 1861, p.434. See Periodical Illustrations 9:xxiv.

54. **Mrs Semple Garrett,** ***Our Little Sunbeam's Picture-Book – Tales and Sketches.*** George Routledge and Sons, 1877. [12805.l.16]

Page 25 is a reprint of 'Swing Song' from *Once a Week*, 1861, p.434. Here it is re-titled 'Tommy's Swing'. See no.53 above.

1878

55. Henry Frith, *Little Valentine and other tales.* George Routledge and Sons, 1878. [12809.cc.33]

Reprint facing page 61, 'Swing Song' from *Once a Week*, 1861, p.434. See no.53 above.

56. Byron, *Poetical Works.* Frederick Warne and Co., Landsdowne Poets series [?1878]. [BM – de Beaumont Collection 1992-4-6-49]

Reprint facing page 74, 'The Dream' from Willmott's *Poets of the Nineteenth Century* (1857). See no.7 above.

1879

57. William Makepeace Thackeray, *The Memoirs of Barry Lyndon, Esq.…and The Fatal Boots.* Volume xix in the de luxe complete edition, Smith, Elder and Co., 1879. [LR.50.c & d]

Four wood-engravings by Joseph Swain after Millais:

(i) Facing page 15. 'A Rhyme for Aristotle'. 100 × 136 mm (4 × 5⅜ in).

(ii) Facing page 18. 'Barry Lyndon's First Love'. 127 × 103 mm (5 × 4 in).

(iii) Facing page 207. 'The Intercepted Letters'. 133 × 99 mm (5¼ × 3⅞ in).

(iv) Facing page 287. 'The Last Days of Barry Lyndon'. 133 × 101 mm (5¼ × 4 in).

58. *By the Etching Club.* 1879. [V&A 29325.13]

Etching , 'A Penny For her Thoughts'. Signed in monogram, dated '1878' and numbered '13' in the plate. 252 × 185 mm (9⅞ × 7¼ in). Image 204 × 170 (8 × 6¾ in).

Geoffroy Millais is confident that the print shows the artist's second daughter, Mary Hunt Millais (1860–1944).

1880

59. Harriet Martineau, *The Hampdens.* Routledge and Sons, 1880 [1879] [12641.c.16]

Ten wood-engravings by Joseph Swain after Millais. Reprints from *Once a Week*, 1863. See Periodical Illustrations 9:xlix–lviii.

60. Mrs Lucy Sale Barker, *Little Wide-Awake Poetry Book for Children.* Routledge and Sons [1880]. [12809.dd.9]

Reprint on page 71 of 'Practising', from *Once a Week*, 10 March 1860, p.242. See Periodical Illustrations 9:xii.

1881

61. Lisbeth Gooch Séguin (afterwards Strahan), *Rural England.* Strahan and Co. [1881]. [14001.g.36]

Reprints from *Saint Pauls* and *Good Words*.

De luxe edition on hand-made paper, with proofs on Japanese paper. Limited edition of 600 copies. Printed by the Dalziel Brothers.

(i) Page 167. 'Going out to Dinner', reprint of 'One kiss before we part' from *Saint Pauls* (*Phineas Finn*; Periodical Illustrations 12:i).

(ii) Page 168. 'The Hunt Ball', reprint of 'You ought to have known. Of course she is in town' from *Saint Pauls* (*Phineas Finn*; Periodical Illustrations 12:xi).

(iii) Page 169. 'Squire Talbot at Home', reprint of 'And I ain't in a hurry either – am I Mamma?' from *Saint Pauls* (*Phineas Finn*; Periodical Illustrations 12:xvi).

(iv) Page 180. 'Theodora', reprint of 'Oh the lark is singing in the sky' from *Good Words* (Periodical Illustrations 5:xvi).

1882

62. **Anthony Trollope, *Kept in the Dark*.** The Piccadilly Novels, Chatto and Windus, 1882. Two volumes. [12643.b.15]

Frontispiece. Wood-engraving by Joseph Swain after Millais. A reduced reprint of the illustration in *Good Words*, 1882: see Periodical Illustrations 5:xxii. 146 × 96 mm (5¾ × 3¾ in).

1883

63. **Henry Leslie, *Leslie's Songs for Little Folks*.** Cassell and Co. [1883]. [BL Music Library B.407.a]

Reprint of *Little Songs for Me to Sing* (1865), see no.32 above. This book, however, contains a new frontispiece illustration apparently engraved by Ahyer of a nun gazing out of her convent window. Signed in monogram and dated 1854. There was a reprint by Cramer and Co., also undated (*c.*1885). 109 × 92 mm (4¼ × 3z in).

This is not the same design as the one Millais employed in The Moxon Tennyson (1857; see no.6 above). The original drawing was exhibited in the Arts Council touring exhibition, 'The Drawings of John Everett Millais', Bolton Museum and Art Gallery and elsewhere, 1979 (cat. no.30, reproduced).

64. **George MacDonald, *Paul Faber, Surgeon*.** Chatto and Windus (New Edition), 1883. [Library of Congress PR 4967.138.1883]

Untitled frontispiece. Engraved by Joseph Swain. A reduced reprint of a design from 'Phineas Finn' in *Saint Pauls* entitled 'But you Irish fellows always ride'. For details see Periodical Illustrations 12:vii. 144 × 98 mm (5⅝ × 3⅞ in).

1885

65. **A. Stewart Harrison, *The Queen of the Arena and other Stories*** T. Fisher Unwin [1885]. [12624.L.12]

Wood-engraving facing page 205 by Joseph Swain after Millais. Reprint from *Once a Week*, 1860 p.435. See Periodical Illustrations 9:xix.

1889

66. **William Allingham, *Life and Phantasy*.** Reeves and Turner, 1889. [01658.f.27]

The frontispiece is a reprint of Millais's design for *The Music Master...* (1855). See no.3 above.

1892

67. **John Guille Millais, *Game Birds and Shooting Sketches....*** Henry Sotheran and Co., 1892. [7285.k.10]

An autotype reproduction of a drawing of Thomas Bewick printed in brown, signed in monogram and dated 1891. 250 × 178 mm (9⅞ × 7 in).

1895

68. **John Guille Millais, *A Breath from the Veldt.*** Henry Sotheran and Co., 1895. [L.R.404.d.7]

Frontispiece electro-etching by Millais entitled 'The Last Trek'. Signed in monogram and dated 1895. 149 × 220 mm (5⅞ × 8⅝ in).

1901

69. **John Guille Millais, *The Wildfowler in Scotland.*** Longmans, Green and Co., 1901. [7905.K.21]

Frontispiece photogravure after a design by Millais, 'The Morning Flight'. 214 × 147 mm (8⅜ × 5¾ in).

no date

70. **Wace, *Ses Oeuvres.*** [BM 1877-8-11-1429]

Engraved by Swain after Millais, apparently for a projected work by John Sullivan of Jersey. The book does not appear to have reached publication, although proofs are to be found in several public collections. 140 × 108 mm (5½ × 4¼ in).

THE PERIODICAL ILLUSTRATIONS

1. THE ARGOSY [Pp6004 gs]

(i) 'The Sighing of the Shell', June 1866, facing page 64. Engraved by Dalziel. 113 × 95 mm (4½ × 3¾ in). Poem by George MacDonald.

2. THE MAGAZINE OF ART [Pp1931 pci]

(i) 'The Fair Maidens', 1878, frontispiece. Engraved by Swain. 188 × 138 mm (7⅜ × 5⅜ in). Reprinted as 'These Twin Girls', in *The Sunday Magazine*, 1883.

(ii) Facing page 54 in the latter section of the magazine of 1878 is a further engraving by Swain after a painting by Millais: 'The North-West Passage' or 'It might be done and England ought to do it'. 137 × 174 mm (5⅜ × 6⅞ in).

3. THE CHURCHMAN'S FAMILY MAGAZINE [Pp357 b]

(i) 'Let that be, please!', January 1863, facing page 15.

(ii) 'You will forgive me, won't you? said Ralph', February 1863, facing page 221.

Both engraved by Joseph Swain after Millais. To 'The New Curate'. each 177 × 113 mm (7 × 4½ in).

4. THE CORNHILL MAGAZINE [Pp 6004 gk]

(i) 'Unspoken Dialogue', February 1860, facing page 194. Engraved by Dalziel. 158 × 108 mm (6¼ × 4¼ in). Poem by R. Monkton Milnes.

(ii) 'Lord Lufton and Lucy Robarts', April 1860, facing page 449. Engraved by Dalziel. 152 × 98 mm (6 × 3⅞ in). To Anthony Trollope, *Framley Parsonage.*

(iii) 'Was it not a lie?', June 1860, facing page 691. Engraved by Dalziel. 171 × 112 mm (6¾ × 4⅜ in). To Anthony Trollope, *Framley Parsonage.*

(iv) 'The Crawley Family', August 1860, facing page 129. Engraved by Dalziel. 169 × 112 mm (6⅝ × 4⅜ in). To Anthony Trollope, *Framley Parsonage.*

(v) 'Lady Lufton and the Duke of Omnium', October 1860, facing page 462. Engraved by Dalziel. 172 × 112 mm (6¾ × 4⅜ in). To Anthony Trollope, *Framley Parsonage.*

(vi) 'Last Words', November 1860, facing page 513. Engraved by Dalziel. 150 × 113 mm (5⅞ × 4½ in). Poem by Owen Meredith.

(vii) 'Mrs Gresham and Miss Dunstable', January 1861, facing page 48. Engraved by Dalziel. 163 × 112 mm (6⅜ × 4⅜ in). To Anthony Trollope, *Framley Parsonage.*

(viii) 'Temptation', February 1861, facing page 229. Engraved by Dalziel. 167 × 114 mm (6⅝ × 4½ in). To 'Horace Saltoun'.

(ix) '"Mark" she said "the men are here"', March 1861, facing page 342. Engraved by Dalziel. 175 × 111 mm (6⅞ × 4⅜ in). To Anthony Trollope, *Framley Parsonage.*

(x) 'Irené', April 1862, facing page 478. Engraved by Joseph Swain. 173 × 114 mm (6¾ × 4½ in). To 'Irené'. The poem is signed 'RM'.

(xi) 'The Bishop and the Knight', July 1862, facing page 100. Engraved by Dalziel. 175 × 108 mm (6⅞ × 4¼ in). The poem is signed 'M'.

(xii) 'Please Ma'am, can we have the peas to shell?', September 1862, facing page 364 with an initial letter design on page 364. Engraved by Dalziel. 163 x103 mm (6⅜ × 4 in). To Anthony Trollope, *The Small House at Allington.*

(xiii) '"And you love me!" said she', October 1862, facing page 552 with an initial letter design on page 552. Engraved by Dalziel. 159 × 105 mm (6¼ × 4⅛ in). To Anthony Trollope, *The Small House at Allington.*

(xiv) 'It's all the fault of the naughty birds', November 1862, facing page 663 with an initial letter design on page 663. Engraved by Dalziel. 159 × 103 mm (6¼ × 4 in). To Anthony Trollope, *The Small House at Allington.*

(xv) '"Mr. Cradell, your hand" said Lupex', December 1862, facing page 780 with an initial letter design on page 780. Engraved by Dalziel. 158 × 104 mm (6¼ × 4⅛ in). To Anthony Trollope, *The Small House at Allington.*

(xvi) 'Why, it's young Eames', January 1863, facing page 56 with an initial letter design on page 56. Engraved by Dalziel. 158 × 105 mm (6¼ × 4⅛ in). To Anthony Trollope, *The Small House at Allington.*

(xvii) 'There is Mr. Harding coming out of the Deanery', February 1863, facing page 214 with an initial letter design on page 214. Engraved by Dalziel. 158 × 104 mm (6¼ × 4⅛ in). To Anthony Trollope, *The Small House at Allington.*

(xviii) 'And have I not really loved you?', March 1863, facing page 349 with an initial letter design on page 349. Engraved by Dalziel. 158 × 104 mm (6¼ × 4⅛ in). To Anthony Trollope, *The Small House at Allington.*

(xix) 'Mr. Palliser and Lady Dumbello', April 1863, facing page 469 with an initial letter design on page 469. Engraved by Dalziel. 160 × 105 mm (6¼ × 4⅛ in). To Anthony Trollope, *The Small House at Allington.*

(xx) 'Devotedly attached to the young man!', May 1863, facing page 657 with an initial letter design on page 657. Engraved by Dalziel. 158 × 106 mm (6¼ × 4⅛ in). To Anthony Trollope, *The Small House at Allington.*

(xxi) 'The Board', June 1863, facing page 756 with an initial letter design on page 756. Engraved by Dalziel. 157 × 104 mm (6⅛ × 4⅛ in). To Anthony Trollope, *The Small House at Allington.*

(xxii) 'Won't you take some more wine?', July 1863, facing page 59 with an initial letter design on page 59. Engraved by Dalziel. 157 × 104 mm (6⅛ × 4⅛ in). To Anthony Trollope, *The Small House at Allington.*

(xxiii) 'And you went in at him on the station?', August 1863, facing page 208 with an initial letter design on page 208. Engraved by Dalziel. 157 × 103 mm (6⅛ × 4 in). To Anthony Trollope, *The Small House at Allington.*

(xxiv) 'Let me beg you to think over the matter again', September 1863, facing page 258 with an initial letter design on page 258. Engraved by Dalziel. 159 × 104 mm (6¼ × 4⅛ in). To Anthony Trollope, *The Small House at Allington.*

(xxv) 'That might do', October 1863, facing page 385 with an initial letter design on page 385. Engraved by Dalziel. 159 × 104 mm (6¼ × 4⅛ in). To Anthony Trollope, *The Small House at Allington.*

(xxvi) '"Mamma" she said at last. "It is all over now, I'm sure"', November 1863, facing page 513 with an initial letter design on page 513. Engraved by Dalziel. 157 × 103 mm (6⅛ × 4 in). To Anthony Trollope, *The Small House at Allington.*

(xxvii) 'Why, on earth, on Sunday?', December 1863, facing page 641 with an initial letter design on page 641. Engraved by Dalziel. 158 × 103 mm (6¼ × 4 in). To Anthony Trollope, *The Small House at Allington.*

(xxviii) 'Bell, here's the inkstand', January 1864, facing page 1 with an initial letter design on page 1. Engraved by Dalziel. 158 × 104 mm (6¼ × 4⅛ in). To Anthony Trollope, *The Small House at Allington.*

(xxix) 'She has refused me and it is all over', February 1864, facing page 232 with an initial letter design on page 232. Engraved by Dalziel. 158 × 104 mm (6¼ × 4⅛ in). To Anthony Trollope, *The Small House at Allington.*

(xxx) Untitled initial letter illustration, April 1864, page 442. Engraved by Dalziel. To Anthony Trollope, *The Small House at Allington.*

(xxxi) 'An Old Song', October 1864, facing page 434 with an initial letter design on page 434. Engraved by Dalziel. 161 × 104 mm (6⅜ × 4⅛ in). To 'Madame de Monferrato'.

5. GOOD WORDS [Pp 6214 d]

(i) 'Olaf the Sinner and Olaf the Saint', January 1862, page 25. Engraved by Dalziel. 88 × 127 mm (3½ × 5 in). The story is signed 'H.K.'

(ii) Untitled frontispiece, 1862. Engraved by Dalziel. 152 × 113 mm (6 × 4½ in). To Dinah Mulock (Mrs Craik), *Mistress and Maid.* Reprinted in *Collected Illustrations*, 1866, no.13 (Book Illustrations 38).

(iii) Untitled illustration, January 1862, page 33. Engraved by Dalziel. 151 × 113 mm (6 × 4½ in). To Dinah Mulock (Mrs Craik), *Mistress and Maid.* Reprinted in *Collected Illustrations*, 1866, no.71 (Book Illustrations 38).

(iv) Untitled illustration, February 1862, page 97. Engraved by Dalziel. 152 × 113 mm (6 × 4½ in). To Dinah Mulock (Mrs Craik), *Mistress and Maid.* Reprinted in *Collected Illustrations*, 1866, no.58 (Book Illustrations 38). The design was reworked by Millais for the steel-engraved frontispiece to the Hurst and Blackett *Standard Library* edition. See Book Illustrations 17.

(v) Untitled illustration, March 1862, page 161. Engraved by Dalziel. 152 × 113 mm (6 × 4½ in). To Dinah Mulock (Mrs Craik), *Mistress and Maid.*

(vi) Untitled illustration, April 1862, page 225. Engraved by Dalziel. 152 × 113 mm (6 × 4½ in). To Dinah Mulock (Mrs Craik), *Mistress and Maid*. Reprinted in *Collected Illustrations*, 1866, no.67 (Book Illustrations 38).

(vii) Untitled illustration, May 1862, page 289. Engraved by Dalziel. 153 × 114 mm (6 × 4½ in). To Dinah Mulock (Mrs Craik), *Mistress and Maid*. Reprinted in *Collected Illustrations*, 1866, no.64 (Book Illustrations 38).

(viii) Untitled illustration, June 1862, page 353. Engraved by Dalziel. 152 × 113 mm (64 × 4½ in). To Dinah Mulock (Mrs Craik), *Mistress and Maid*. Reprinted in *Collected Illustrations*, 1866, no.39 (Book Illustrations 38).

(ix) Untitled illustration, July 1862, page 417. Engraved by Dalziel. 151 × 113 mm (6 × 4½ in). To Dinah Mulock (Mrs Craik), *Mistress and Maid*.

(x) Untitled illustration, August 1862, page 481. Engraved by Dalziel. 152 × 113 mm (6 × 4½ in). To Dinah Mulock (Mrs Craik), *Mistress and Maid*. Reprinted in *Collected Illustrations*, 1866, no.69 (Book Illustrations 38).

(xi) Untitled illustration, September 1862, page 545. Engraved by Dalziel. 152 × 113 mm (6 × 4½ in). To Dinah Mulock (Mrs Craik), *Mistress and Maid*. Reprinted in *Collected Illustrations*, 1866, no.12 (Book Illustrations 38).

(xii) Untitled illustration, October 1862, page 609. Engraved by Dalziel. 151 × 113 mm (6 × 4½ in). To Dinah Mulock (Mrs Craik), *Mistress and Maid*. Reprinted in *Collected Illustrations*, 1866, no.60. (Book Illustrations 38).

(xiii) Untitled illustration, November 1862, page 673. Engraved by Dalziel. 153 × 113 mm (6 × 4½ in). To Dinah Mulock (Mrs Craik), *Mistress and Maid*.

(xiv) 'Highland Flora', July 1862, page 393. Engraved by Dalziel. 107 × 130 mm (4¼ × 5⅛ in).

(xv) Twelve illustrations to *The Parables of Our Lord*, 1863. These appeared monthly. Engraved by Dalziel. Placed as frontispiece ('The Labourers in the Vineyard', referring to text on page 821) and facing pages 1, 81, 161, 241, 313, 385, 461, 533, 605, 677 and 749. For details see Book Illustrations 25. 'The Unjust Judge' and 'The Ten Virgins' are reprinted in *Collected Illustrations*, 1866, nos 38 and 54 respectively (Book Illustrations 38).

(xvi) 'O the lark is singing in the sky', January 1864, facing page 64. Engraved by Swain. 147 × 112 mm (5¾ × 4⅜ in). The poem is signed 'R.B.R.' Reprinted in *Collected Illustrations*, 1866, no.37 (Book Illustrations 38).

(xvii) 'A Scene for a Study', February 1864, facing page 160. Engraved by Swain. 140 × 109 mm (5½ × 4¼ in). Poem by Jean Ingelow.

(xviii) 'Polly', March 1864, facing page 248. Engraved by Swain. 159 × 115 mm (6¼ × 4½ in). Reprinted in *Collected Illustrations*, 1866, no.30 (Book Illustrations 38).

(xix) 'The Bridal of Dandelot', April 1864, facing page 304. Engraved by Swain. 158 × 114 mm (6¼ × 4½ in). Reprinted in *Collected Illustrations*, 1866, no.55 (Book Illustrations 38). Poem by Dora Greenwell.

(xx) 'Prince Philibert', June 1864, facing page 481. Engraved by Swain. 157 × 110 mm (6⅛ × 4⅜ in). Reprinted in *Collected Illustrations*, 1866, no.17 (Book Illustrations 38).

(xxi) 'Macleod of Dare', September 1878, facing page 651. Engraved by Swain. 91 × 136 mm (3⅜ × 5⅜ in). Text by William Black.

(xxii) 'Kept in the Dark', probably to accompany April 1882, frontispiece or facing page 365. Engraved by Swain. 163 × 110 mm (6⅜ × 4⅜ in). See also Book Illustrations 62. To Anthony Trollope, *Kept in the Dark*.

6. THE ILLUSTRATED LONDON NEWS [Pp 7611]

(i) 'Christmas Story-Telling', 20 December 1862. Presented separately in the magazine (no page). Engraved by Dalziel. 239 × 347 mm (9⅜ × 13⅝ in). Accompanies no text. The proof in the Dalziel Archive in the British Museum is touched by the artist.

7. THE INFANT'S MAGAZINE [Pp 5992 ga]

(i) 'The Picture-Book', no. 23, 1 November 1867 page 175. No engraver's name. A reprint of the title-page vignette, which first appears in Wordsworth's *Poems for the Young* (1863). See Book Illustrations 20.

8. LONDON SOCIETY [Pp 6004 gp]

(i) 'Ah Me! She was a winsome maid', August 1862, facing page 181. Engraved by Dalziel. 188 × 117 mm (7⅜ × 4⅝ in). To 'The Border Witch', a poem subtitled 'An Auld-Warld Story' and signed 'TW'.

(ii) '"Yes, Lewis," she said; "Quite satisfied"', Christmas number 1862, facing page 65. Engraved by Swain. 186 × 113 mm (7⅜ × 4½ in). To 'The Christmas Wreaths of Rockton'.

(iii) 'Knightly Worth', September 1864, facing page 193. Engraved by Dalziel. 184 × 113 mm (7¼ × 4½ in). To 'The Tale of a Chivalrous Life': usually placed as a frontispiece to the 1864 bound volume but in some copies placed opposite the story facing page 247.

9. ONCE A WEEK [Pp 6004 gi]

(i) 'Magenta', 2 July 1859, page 10. Engraved by Dalziel. 85 × 79 mm (3⅜ × 3⅛ in). Poem by Tom Taylor.

(ii) 'The Grandmother's Apology', 16 July 1859, page 41. Engraved by Dalziel. 99 × 123 mm (3⅞ × 4⅞ in). Reprinted in *Collected Illustrations*, 1866, no.2 (Book Illustrations 38). Poem by Tennyson.

(iii) 'On the Water', 23 July 1859, page 70. Engraved by Dalziel. 75 × 123 mm (3 × 4⅞ in). Reprinted in *Collected Illustrations*, 1866, no.4. (Book Illustrations 38). Poem signed 'Memor'.

(iv) 'La Fille Bien gardée', 8 October 1859, page 306. Engraved by Swain. 102 × 84 mm (4 × 3¼ in). Reprinted in *Collected Illustrations*, 1866, no.20 (Book Illustrations 38). Poem signed 'SB', with the address 'Queen's Bar Ride, Temple'.

Robin de Beaumont has provided information from the BM Millais Album (1992-4-6-297 [45]) that the sitter is a Miss Eyre and the dog, an Irish wolfhound, was Millais's own, called Roswell. See J.G. Millais, *The Life and Letters of John Everett Millais P.R.A*, 1899, pp.309, 493.

(v) 'The Plague of Elliant', 15 October 1859, page 316. Engraved by Swain. 77 × 128 mm (3 × 5 in). Poem translated from the Breton by Tom Taylor. Reprinted in Taylor's *Ballads and Songs of Brittany*, 1865 (Book Illustrations 30). Also reprinted in *Collected Illustrations*, 1866, no.29 (Book Illustrations 38).

(vi) 'Maude Clare', 5 November 1859, page 382. Engraved by Swain. 101 × 126 mm (4 × 5 in). Reprinted in *Collected Illustrations*, 1866, no.68 (Book Illustrations 38). Poem by Christina Rossetti.

(vii) 'A Lost Love', 3 December 1859, page 482. Engraved by Dalziel. 101 × 83 mm (4 × 3¼ in). Poem signed 'R.A.B.'

Robin de Beaumont has suggested that the sitter may perhaps be Alice Gray, who was the younger of Effie's two surviving sisters (1845–1929). Millais made a watercolour of the subject, now in the British Museum (1937-4-10-3).

(viii) 'St. Bartholomew', 17 December 1859, page 514. Engraved by Dalziel. 76 × 128 mm (3 × 5 in). Reprinted in *Collected Illustrations*, 1866, no.42 (Book Illustrations 38). Poem signed 'H.E.E.M'.

(ix) 'The Crown of Love', 31 December 1859, page 10. Engraved by Swain. 128 × 77 mm (5 × 3 in). Poem by George Meredith.

Geoffroy Millais has kindly pointed out that Millais made an oil painting of this subject in 1875 for which the sitter was Alice Millais (1862–1936), the artist's third daughter.

(x) 'A Wife', 7 January 1860, page 32. Engraved by Swain. 75 × 120 mm (3 × 4¾ in). Poem signed 'A'.

(xi) 'The Head of Bran', 4 February 1860, page 132. Engraved by Swain. 113 × 128 mm (4½ × 5 in). Reprinted in *Collected Illustrations*, 1866, no.16 (Book Illustrations 38). Poem by George Meredith.

(xii) 'Practising', 10 March 1860, page 242. Engraved by Dalziel. 101 × 84 mm (4 × 3¼ in). Poem by Shirley Brooks.

Robin de Beaumont has identified the sitter as Alice Gray from an annotation in the Millais Album (BM 1992-4-6-297 [44]).

(xiii) 'Musa', 16 June 1860, page 598. Engraved by Dalziel. 97 × 83 mm (3⅞ × 3¼ in). Poem signed 'E.M.B'.

Robin de Beaumont has identified the sitters from an annotation in the Millais Album in the British Museum (1992-4-6-297 [42]) as Effie's younger sister Sophia (Sophie) Gray (1843–82) with Millais' eldest sons, Everett (1856–97) and George (1857–78).

(xiv) 'Master Olaf', 14 July 1860, page 63. Engraved by Swain. 102 × 125 mm (4 × 4⅞ in). From the German, the poem is signed 'L.B.'.

(xv) 'Violet', 28 July 1860, page 140. Engraved by Swain. 101 × 82 mm (4 × 3¼ in). Poem by Arthur J. Munby.

Robin de Beaumont has identified the sitter as the artist's wife, Effie (1828–97), from both an original drawing (private collection) and an album of proofs in the British Museum (BM 1992-4-6-297 [41]) that had belonged to the artist. In the latter the design is dated 1855.

(xvi) 'Dark Gordon's Bride', 25 August 1860, page 238. Engraved by Swain. 115 × 126 mm (4½ × 5 in). Reprinted in *Collected Illustrations*, 1866, no.27 (Book Illustrations 38). Poem by B.S. Montgomery.

(xvii) 'The Meeting', 1 September 1860, page 276. Engraved by Swain. 87 × 85 mm (3⅜ × 3¼ in). Reprinted in *Collected Illustrations*, 1866, no.59 (Book Illustrations 38). Poem signed 'G.M.'.

(xviii) 'The Iceberg', 6 October 1860, page 407. Engraved by Swain. 101 × 127 mm (4 × 5 in). Text by A. Stewart Harrison. See also Book Illustrations 65.

(xix) 'The Iceberg', 13 October 1860, page 435. Engraved by Swain. 101 × 127 mm (4 x5 in). Text by A. Stewart Harrison. See also Book Illustrations 65.

(xx) 'A Head of Hair for Sale', 3 November 1860, page 519. Engraved by Swain. 114 × 94 mm (4½ × 3¾ in). Unsigned story.

(xxi) 'Iphis and Anaxarete', 19 January 1861, page 98. Engraved by Swain. 76 × 126 mm (3 × 5 in). Poem by Mary C.F. Münster.

(xxii) 'Thorr's hunt for his Hammer', 26 January 1861, page 126. Engraved by Swain. 77 × 125 mm (3 × 4⅞ in). Poem signed 'G.W.D.'.

(xxiii) 'Tannhaüser', 17 August 1861, page 211. Engraved by Swain. 113 × 93 mm (4½ × 3¾ in). The translated poem is signed 'L.D.G.'.

(xxiv) 'Swing Song', 12 October 1861, page 434. Engraved by Swain. 126 × 74 mm (5 × 2⅞ in). Unsigned poem.

Robin de Beaumont has identified the subject as Everett Millais, the artist's son, from an annotation in the British Museum Millais Album (1992-4-6-297 [43]).

(xxv) 'Schwerting of Saxony', 4 January 1862, page 43. Engraved by Swain. 88 × 127 mm (3½ × 5 in). Poem signed 'A.D.'.

(xxvi) 'The Battle of the Thirty', 1 February 1862, page 155. Engraved by Swain. 114 × 128 mm (4½ × 5 in). An unsigned translation of a Breton ballad. Reprinted in *Collected Illustrations*, 1866, no.45 (Book Illustrations 38).

(xxvii) 'The Fair Jacobite', 22 February 1862, page 239. Engraved by Swain. 113 × 94 mm (4½ × 3¾ in). This is an independent design, apparently not illustrating any particular text. Reprinted in *Collected Illustrations*, 1866, no.35 (Book Illustrations 38).

(xxviii) Untitled illustration, 15 March 1862, page 309. Engraved by Swain. 114 × 126 mm (4½ × 5 in). To Harriet Martineau, *Sister Anna's Probation*. Reprinted in *Collected Illustrations*, 1866, no.25 (Book Illustrations 38), where entitled 'Let us speak together before we sleep'.

(xxix) Untitled illustration, 22 March 1862, page 337. Engraved by Swain. 127 × 100 mm (5 × 4 in). To Harriet Martineau, *Sister Anna's Probation*.

(xxx) Untitled illustration, 29 March 1862, page 365. Engraved by Swain. 129 × 101 mm (5⅛ × 4 in). To Harriet Martineau, *Sister Anna's Probation*. Reprinted in *Collected Illustrations*, 1866, no.44 (Book Illustrations 38), where entitled 'Anna and her lover'.

(xxxi) Untitled illustration, 5 April 1862, page 393. Engraved by Swain. 127 × 100 mm (5 × 4 in). To Harriet Martineau, *Sister Anna's Probation*. Reprinted in *Collected Illustrations*, 1866, no.52 (Book Illustrations 38), where entitled 'Anna rested on her hoe and listened'.

(xxxii) Untitled illustration, 12 April 1862, page 421. Engraved by Swain. 114 × 128 mm (4½ × 5 in). To Harriet Martineau, *Sister Anna's Probation*.

(xxxiii) 'Sir Tristem', 22 March 1862, page 350. Engraved by Swain. 76 × 127 mm (3 × 5 in). Poem by William Buchanan.

(xxxiv) 'The Crusader's Wife', 10 May 1862, page 546. Engraved by Swain. 114 × 94 mm (4½ × 3¾ in). Poem translated from the Breton by Tom Taylor. Reprinted in Taylor's *Ballads and Songs of Brittany*, 1865 (see Book Illustrations 30).

(xxxv) 'The Chase of the Siren', 31 May 1862, page 630. Engraved by Swain. 113 × 94 mm (4½ × 3¾ in). Poem by Walter Thornbury.

(xxxvi) 'The Drowning of Kaer-Is', 14 June 1862, page 687. Engraved by Swain. 112 × 126 mm (4⅜ × 5 in). Poem translated from the Breton by Tom Taylor. Reprinted in Taylor's *Ballads and Songs of Brittany*, 1865 (see Book Illustrations 30). Also reprinted in *Collected Illustrations*, 1866, no.34 (Book Illustrations 38), where entitled 'I will win the key from my father's side'.

(xxxvii) 'Margaret Wilson', 5 July 1862, page 42. Engraved by Swain. 128 × 101 mm (5 × 4 in). Reprinted in *Collected Illustrations*, 1866, no.3 (Book Illustrations 38), where entitled 'Margaret Wilson, the Scottish Martyr'.

(xxxviii) Untitled illustration, 19 July 1862, page 85. Engraved by Swain. 113 × 127 mm (4½ × 5 in). To Harriet Martineau, *The Anglers of the Dove*. The tale (called 'An Historiette') is based on Bess of Hardwick; the Dove referred to in the title is the River Dove. Reprinted in *Collected Illustrations*, 1866, no.74 (Book Illustrations 38), where entitled 'Farmer Chell's Kitchen'.

(xxxix) Untitled illustration, 26 July 1862, page 113. Engraved by Swain. 127 × 98 mm (5 × 3⅞ in). To Harriet Martineau, *The Anglers of the Dove*. Reprinted in *Collected Illustrations*, 1866, no.51 (Book Illustrations 38), where entitled 'Sorting the prey'.

(xl) Untitled illustration, 2 August 1862 , page 141. Engraved by Swain. 113 × 128 mm (4½ × 5 in). To Harriet Martineau, *The Anglers of the Dove*. Reprinted in *Collected Illustrations*, 1866, no.14 (Book Illustrations 38), where entitled 'Mary Queen of Scots at Buxton'.

(xli) Untitled illustration, 9 August 1862, page 169. Engraved by Swain. 102 × 127 mm (4 × 5 in). To Harriet Martineau, *The Anglers of the Dove*.

(xlii) Untitled illustration, 16 August 1862, page 197. Engraved by Swain. 114 × 94 mm (4½ × 3¾ in). To Harriet Martineau, *The Anglers of the Dove*.

(xliii) 'Maid Avoraine', 19 July 1862, page 98. Engraved by Swain. 94 × 114 mm (3¾ × 4½ in). Poem by R. Williams Buchanan.

(xliv) 'The Mite of Dorcas', 16 August 1862, page 224. Engraved by Swain. 122 × 76 mm (4¾ × 3 in). This does not appear to relate to any text in the magazine. Reprinted in *Collected Illustrations*, 1866, no 41 (Book Illustrations 38).

(xlv) 'The Spirit of the Vanished Island', 8 November 1862, page 546. Engraved by Swain. 109 × 125 mm (4¼ × 4⅞ in). Poem by Mrs Acton Tindal.

(xlvi) 'The Parting of Ulysses', 6 December 1862, page 658. Engraved by Swain. 114 × 95 mm (4½ × 3¾ in). The text is from Pope's edition of the *Odyssey*.

(xlvii) 'Limerick Bells', 20 December 1862, page 710. Engraved by Swain. 127 × 101 mm (5 × 4 in). Poem by Horace Moule. Reprinted in *Collected Illustrations*, 1866, no.66 (Book Illustrations 38), where entitled 'The Monk'.

(xlviii) 'Endymion on Latmos', 3 January 1863, page 42. Engraved by Swain. 127 × 101 mm (5 × 4 in). Poem signed 'R.N.S.'.

(xlix) Untitled illustration, 14 February 1863, page 211. Engraved by Swain. 101 × 127 mm (4 × 5 in). To Harriet Martineau, *The Hampdens*. Termed an 'Historiette', the novel is about John Hampden and his refusal to submit to the paying of Ship Money.

(l) Untitled illustration, 21 February 1863, page 239. Engraved by Swain. 113 × 127 mm (4½ × 5 in). To Harriet Martineau, *The Hampdens*. Reprinted in *Collected Illustrations*, 1866, no.31 (Book Illustrations 38), where entitled 'Lady Carew and Margaret'.

(li) Untitled illustration, 28 February 1863, page 267. Engraved by Swain. 114 × 127 mm (4½ × 5 in). To Harriet Martineau, *The Hampdens*. Reprinted in *Collected Illustrations*, 1866, no.5 (Book Illustrations 38), where entitled 'A Scene in Merrie England'.

(lii) Untitled illustration, 7 March 1863, page 281. Engraved by Swain. 114 × 127 mm (4½ × 5 in). To Harriet Martineau, *The Hampdens*.

(liii) Untitled illustration, 14 March 1863, page 309. Engraved by Swain. 111 × 126 mm (4⅜ × 5 in). To Harriet Martineau, *The Hampdens*.

(liv) Untitled illustration, 21 March 1863, page 337. Engraved by Swain. 113 × 125 mm (4½ × 4⅞ in). To Harriet Martineau, *The Hampdens*.

(lv) Untitled illustration, 28 March 1863, page 365. Engraved by Swain. 128 × 112 mm (5 × 4⅜ in). To Harriet Martineau, *The Hampdens*.

(lvi) Untitled illustration, 4 April 1863, page 393. Engraved by Swain. 94 × 112 mm (3¾ × 4⅜ in). To Harriet Martineau, *The Hampdens*. Reprinted in *Collected Illustrations*, 1866, no.76 (Book Illustrations 38), where entitled 'Doing Royal Errands in Merrie England'.

(lvii) Untitled illustration, 11 April 1863, page 421. Engraved by Swain. 108 × 127 mm (4¼ × 5 in). To Harriet Martineau, *The Hampdens*.

(lviii) Untitled illustration, 18 April 1863, page 449. Engraved by Swain. 100 × 127mm (4 × 5 in). To Harriet Martineau, *The Hampdens*.

(lix) 'Hacho the Dane or The Bishop's Ransom', 24 October 1863, page 504. Engraved by Swain. 128 × 114 mm (5 × 4½ in). Poem signed 'C.H.W.'.

(lx) Untitled illustration, 24 October 1863, page 491. Engraved by Swain. 114 × 95 mm (4½ × 3¾ in). To Harriet Martineau, *Son Christopher*. Styled an 'Historiette', the tale involves a Protestant family living in Dorset in 1685 and the Monmouth Rebellion.

(lxi) Untitled illustration, 31 October 1863, page 519. Engraved by Swain. 102 × 128 mm (4 × 5 in). To Harriet Martineau, *Son Christopher*.

(lxii) Untitled illustration, 7 November 1863, page 547. Engraved by Swain. 114 × 126 mm (4½ × 5 in). To Harriet Martineau, *Son Christopher*.

(lxiii) Untitled illustration, 14 November 1863, page 575. Engraved by Swain. 101 × 126 mm (4 × 5 in). To Harriet Martineau, *Son Christopher*. Reprinted in *Collected Illustrations*, 1866, no.18 (Book Illustrations 38), where entitled 'Watching their idol as he galloped away'.

(lxiv) Untitled illustration, 21 November 1863, page 603. Engraved by Swain. 114 × 127 mm (4½ × 5 in). To Harriet Martineau, *Son Christopher*.

(lxv) Untitled illustration, 28 November 1863, page 631. Engraved by Swain. 114 × 128 mm (4½ × 5 in). To Harriet Martineau, *Son Christopher*.

(lxvi) Untitled illustration, 5 December 1863, page 659. Engraved by Swain. 126 × 100 mm (5 × 4 in). To Harriet Martineau, *Son Christopher*.

(lxvii) Untitled illustration, 12 December 1863, page 687. Engraved by Swain. 114 × 126 mm (4½ × 5 in). To Harriet Martineau, *Son Christopher*.

(lxviii) 'Death Dealing Arrows', 25 January 1868, page 79. No engraver's name. 138 × 88 mm (5⅜ × 3½ in). Appears to accompany no text.

(lxix) 'Taking his Ease', 25 December 1868 (the Christmas Number, called *Once a Year*), facing page 64. Engraved by Swain. 130 × 98 mm (5⅛ × 3⅞ in). No copy of this number survives in the British Library but there is one in the University of London Library at the callmark PRZ.

10. PUNCH [Pp 5270]

(i) 'It is the Chapeau Blanc, The White Witness', 21 March 1863, page 115. No engraver's name. 112 × 168 mm (4⅜ × 6⅝ in). See Book Illustrations 50 under F.C. Burnand, *Mokeanna! A Treble Temptation* (1873), where the design is reprinted.

11. PUNCH ALMANACK, 1865 [Pp 5276 1-3]

(i) 'Mr. Vandyke Brown, having left the Dress on the Lay Figure carefully arranged, goes out for his usual exercise, and this is how the Boys took advantage of his absence'. Page un-numbered. Engraved by Swain. 114 × 170 mm (4½ × 6¾ in).

(*Saint Pauls* magazine is invariably spelled thus – in full with no apostrophe.) Twenty illustrations, all to Anthony Trollope, *Phineas Finn the Irish Member*, October 1867 to May 1869.

(i) 'One kiss before we part', October 1867, facing page 118. Engraved by Swain. 144 × 102 mm (5⅝ × 4 in).

(ii) 'You don't quite know Mr. Kennedy yet', November 1867, facing page 247. No engraver's name visible but presumably Swain. 150 × 101 mm (5⅞ × 4 in).

(iii) 'I wish you would be in earnest with me', December 1867, facing page 374 or 375. Engraved by Swain. 103 × 157 mm (4 × 6⅛ in).

(iv) 'I wish to regard you as a dear friend, – both of my own and of my husband', January 1868, facing page 509. No engraver's name visible, though presumably Swain. 137 × 105 mm (5⅜ × 4⅛ in).

(v) 'Laura, would you mind leaving me and Miss Effingham alone for a few minutes?', February 1868, facing page 637. Engraved by Swain. 157 × 105 mm (6⅛ × 4⅛ in).

(vi) 'And do be punctual, Mr. Finn', March 1868, facing page 750 or 751. Engraved by Swain. 153 × 104 mm (6 × 4⅛ in).

(vii) 'But you Irish fellows always ride', April 1868, facing page 113. Engraved by Swain. 154 × 105 mm (6⅛ × 4⅛ in).

(viii) 'May I give him your love?', May 1868, facing page 253. Engraved by Swain. 154 × 105 mm (6⅛ × 4⅛ in).

(ix) 'I will send for Dr. Macnuthrie at once', June 1868, facing page 376 or 377. Engraved by Swain. 103 × 156 mm (4 × 6⅛ in).

(x) 'I do not choose that there should be a riot here', July 1868, facing page 510 or 511. No engraver's name visible but presumably Swain. 153 × 103 mm (6 × 4 in).

(xi) 'You ought to have known. Of course she is in town', August 1868, facing page 638. Engraved by Swain. 157 × 104 mm (6⅛ × 4⅛ in).

(xii) 'It's the system as I hates, and not you, Mr. Finn', September 1868, facing page 747. Engraved by Swain. 157 × 103 mm (6⅛ × 4 in).

(xiii) 'The fact is, mamma, I love him', October 1868, facing page 128. Engraved by Swain. 158 × 105 mm (6¼ × 4⅛ in).

(xiv) 'So she burned the morsel of paper', November 1868, facing page 233. Engraved by Swain. 157 × 105 mm (6⅛ × 4⅛ in).

(xv) 'You must come', December 1868, facing page 381. Engraved by Swain. 156 × 104 mm (6⅛ × 4⅛ in).

(xvi) 'And I ain't in a hurry either, – am I, Mamma?', January 1869, facing either page 502 or 503. Engraved by Swain. 157 × 104 mm (6⅛ × 4⅛ in).

(xvii) 'Phineas had no alternative but to read the letter', February 1869, facing page 636 (incorrectly placed in the British Library copy facing page 626). Engraved by Swain. 157 × 105 mm (6⅛ × 4⅛ in).

(xviii) 'I mean what I say. Why should I care?', March 1869, facing page 738 or 739. Engraved by Swain. 157 × 104 mm (6⅛ × 4⅛ in).

(xix) 'Ever your own, with all the love of her heart, Mary F. Jones', April 1869, facing page 103. Engraved by Swain. 157 × 104 mm (6⅛ × 4⅛ in).

(xx) 'Oh, Phineas; surely a thousand a year will be very nice.', May 1869, facing page 256. Engraved by Swain. 158 × 103 mm (6¼ × 4 in).

SELECT BIBLIOGRAPHY

Anon., Review of *The Parables of Our Lord* in *The Athenaeum*, no.1867, 26 December 1863, pp.881–2.

Dalziel Brothers, *The Brothers Dalziel: A Record*, London: Methuen and Co., 1901 (reprint London: Batsford, 1978, with an introduction by Graham Reynolds).

Engen, Rodney, *Dictionary of Victorian Wood Engravers*, Cambridge: Chadwyck-Healey, 1985.

Engen, Rodney, *Pre-Raphaelite Prints*, London: Lund Humphries, 1995.

Exhibition Catalogue, *The Woodcut Illustrations of Millais*, introduction by C.J. Holmes, London: Hacon and Ricketts, 1898.

Exhibition Catalogue, *Millais*, London: Royal Academy of Arts and Liverpool: Walker Art Gallery, 1967.

Exhibition Catalogue, *Pre-Raphaelite Graphics*, London: Hartnoll and Eyre Ltd, 1974.

Exhibition Catalogue, *The Drawings of John Everett Millais*, Arts Council, Bolton: Bolton Museum and Art Gallery and elsewhere, 1979.

Exhibition Catalogue, *John Everett Millais 1829–1896: A Centenary Exhibition*, Southampton: Southampton Institute, 1996.

Fredeman, William E., *Pre-Raphaelitism: A Bibliocritical Study*, Cambridge, Mass.: Harvard University Press, 1965.

Goldman, Paul, *Victorian Illustrated Books 1850–1870: The Heyday of Wood-Engraving*, London: British Museum Press, 1994.

Goldman, Paul, *Victorian Illustration: The Pre-Raphaelites, The Idyllic School and the High Victorians*, London: Lund Humphries, 2004 (revised edition).

Goldman, Paul, 'A Consummate Illustrator: John Everett Millais' in *Singular Visions*, Imaginative Book Illustration Society Journal 2, 2002, pp.37–51.

Hall, N. John, *Trollope and His Illustrators*, London: The Macmillan Press, 1980.

Hardie, Martin, *Catalogue of Prints: Wood Engravings after Sir John Everett Millais, Bart., P.R.A. in the Victoria and Albert Museum*, London: Victoria and Albert Museum, 1908.

Layard, George Somes, 'Millais and *Once a Week*' in *Good Words*, August 1893, pp.552–8.

Layard, George Somes, *Tennyson and his Pre-Raphaelite Illustrators*, London: Elliot Stock, 1894.

Life, Allan Roy, 'Art and Poetry: A Study of the Illustrations of Two Pre-Raphaelite Artists, William Holman Hunt and John Everett Millais', unpublished doctoral thesis, University of British Columbia, 1974.

Life, Allan Roy , 'The Periodical Illustrations of John Everett Millais and their Literary Interpretation' in *Victorian Periodicals Newsletter* 9, June 1976, pp.50–68.

Lutyens, Mary (ed.), 'Letters from Sir John Everett Millais ... and William Holman Hunt in the Henry E. Huntington Library, San Marino, California' in *Walpole Society*, vol.44, 1972–4, pp.1–93.

Lutyens, Mary (intro.), *The Parables of Our Lord and Saviour Jesus Christ with Pictures by John Everett Millais*, New York: Dover Publications, 1975.

Mason, Michael, 'The way we look now: Millais' illustrations to Trollope' in *Art History*, vol.1 no.3, September 1978, pp.309–40.

Millais, John Guille, *The Life and Letters of Sir John Everett Millais P.R.A.*, London: Methuen and Co., 1899.

Munro, Jane, *Tennyson and Trollope: Book Illustrations by John Everett Millais (1829–1896)*, Cambridge: Fitzwilliam Museum, 1996.

Oakley, Maroussia, 'John Everett Millais and the elusive Maggy Band' in *Burlington Magazine*, vol.CXLVI, no.1210 (January 2004), p.30.

Pennell, Joseph and E.R., 'John Everett Millais, Painter and Illustrator' in *Fortnightly Review*, n.s. vol.LX, July–December 1896 (o.s. vol.LXVI), pp.443–50.

Reid, Forrest, *Illustrators of the Sixties*, London: Faber and Gwyer, 1928.

Sadleir, Michael, *Trollope: A Bibliography*, Folkestone: William Dawson, 1977 (reprint of the edition first published in 1928).

Suriano, Gregory R., *The Pre-Raphaelite Illustrators: The Published Graphic Art of the English Pre-Raphaelites and their Associates*, New Castle, Delaware: Oak Knoll Press and London: The British Library, 2000.

Ullmann, Jennifer M., '"The Perfect Delineation of Character": Process and Perfection in the Book Illustrations of John Everett Millais' in *Pocket Cathedrals: Pre-Raphaelite Book Illustration* (ed. Susan P. Casteras), New Haven: Yale Center for British Art, 1991, pp.55–65.

Vaughan, William, 'Incongruous Disciples: The Pre-Raphaelites and the Moxon Tennyson' in *Imagination on a Long Rein: English Literature Illustrated* (ed. Joachim Moller), Marburg: Jonas Verlag, 1988, pp.148–60.

PLATES

The Book Illustrations

The illustrations are wood-engraved unless stated otherwise, using digital scans taken directly from the original images in the books and periodicals. The wood-engravings were usually scanned in line, with half-tone for the etchings and steel engravings. They are all reproduced actual size, as far as has proved possible. It should also be noted that the measurements of the etchings given in the Catalogue of Illustrations are to the plate marks (where visible) and to the images; all other measurements are to the image only.

1. 'St. Agnes of Intercession', [1850]

2. *Mr. Wray's Cash-Box*, 1852

1. 'St. Agnes of Intercession', *etching*:

Intended for the fifth number of *The Germ* but never published. It was to have accompanied a story by Dante Gabriel Rossetti, about a contemporary artist who discovers that he is, in reality, a reincarnation of a fifteenth century painter, Bucciuolo Angiolieri. Millais's scene concerns an episode involving Bucciuolo and his lover Blanzifiore dall' Ambra which the artist reads about in a catalogue. She is taken fatally ill in Lucca and summons Bucciuolo to rush to her deathbed from Florence.

'When, on his arrival, she witnessed his anguish at thus losing her forever, Blanzifiore declared at once that she would rise from her bed, and that Bucciuolo should paint her portrait before she died; for so, she said, there should still remain something to him whereby to have her in memory. In this will she persisted against all remonstrance occasioned by the fears of her friends ; and for two days, though in a dying state, she sat with wonderful energy to her lover clad in her most sumptuous attire, and arrayed with all her jewels: her two sisters remaining constantly at her side, to sustain her, and supply restoratives. On the third day, while Bucciuolo was still at work, she died without moving.'

2. W. Wilkie Collins, *Mr. Wray's Cash-Box; or, The Mask and the Mystery. A Christmas Sketch.* 1852. *Etched frontispiece:*

Annie Wray ties her lover, Martin Blunt's cravat: '... telling him to stoop, [she] tied his cravat directly – standing on tiptoe'.

3. *The Music Master*, 1855 4. *The Pleasures of Home*, [1855/6]

3. William Allingham, *The Music Master, A Love Song, and two series of Day and Night Songs*, 1855.

'Frost in the Holidays': 'Little Caroline ... Has stolen her fingers up into mine.'

4. Reverend John Anderson, *The Pleasures of Home: A Poem in Two Parts*, [1855/6]

'The Long-Lost son Revisits Childhood's Home'.

5. Thomas Moore, *Irish Melodies*, 1856.

'When first I met thee', *steel-engraving*:

> 'When first I met thee, warm and young,
> There shone such truth about thee, ...
> I did not dare to doubt thee.'

5. *Irish Melodies*, 1856

6. Alfred Tennyson, *Poems*, 1857.

(i) 'Mariana': 'I would that I were dead!'

(ii) 'The Miller's Daughter': 'Yet fill my glass: give me one kiss:
My own sweet Alice, we must die.'

(iii) 'The Miller's Daughter': 'As near this door you sat apart,
And rose, and with a silent grace
Approaching, press'd you heart to heart.'

(iv) 'The Sisters': 'The wind is blowing in turret and tree.'

6. Tennyson, *Poems*, 1857

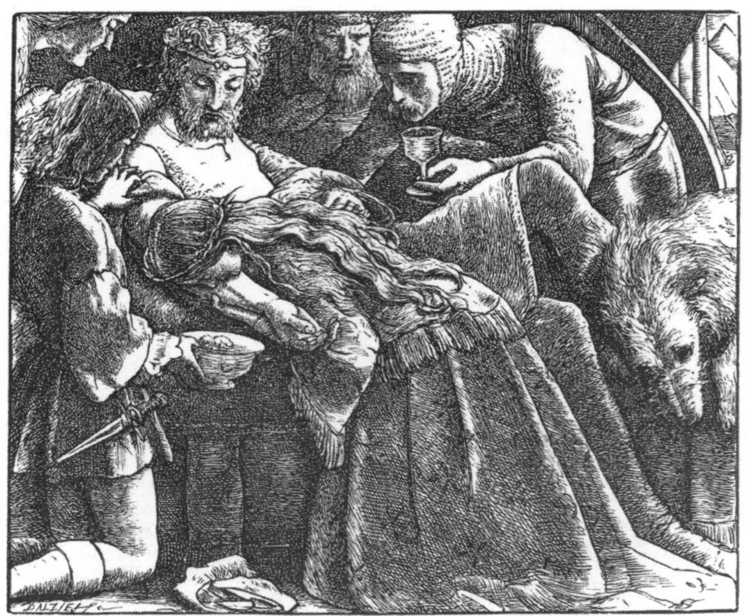

(v) 'A Dream of Fair Women': '(With that she tore her robe apart, and half
The polish'd argent of her breast to sight
Laid bare. Thereto she pointed with a laugh,
Showing the aspick's bite)'

(vi) 'A Dream of Fair Women': 'Or her, who knew that Love can vanquish Death,
Who kneeling, with one arm about her king,
Drew forth the poison with her balmy breath,
Sweet as new buds in Spring.'

(vii) 'The Death of the Old Year': 'Toll ye the church-bell sad and slow,'

(viii) 'Dora': '... Then the old man
Was wroth, and doubled up his hands, and said:
"You will not, boy! you dare to answer thus !"'

6. Tennyson, *Poems*, 1857

(ix) 'Dora': '... Then they clung about
The old man's neck, and kissed him many times.
And all the man was broken with remorse;'

(x) 'The Talking Oak': 'Tho' what he whisper'd, under Heaven
None else could understand;
I found him garrulously given,
A babbler in the land.'

(xi) 'The Talking Oak': 'And when my marriage morn may fall,
She, Dryad-like, shall wear
Alternate leaf and acorn-ball
In wreath about her hair.'

(xii) 'Locksley Hall': 'Saying "Dost thou love me, cousin?" weeping,
"I have loved thee long."'

6. Tennyson, *Poems*, 1857

(xiii) 'Locksley Hall': Unusually, it is difficult to perceive with accuracy exactly which point in the poem is being illustrated.

(xiv) 'St. Agnes' Eve': 'Deep on the convent-roof the snows
Are sparkling to the moon:
My breath to heaven like vapour goes:
May my soul follow soon!'

(xv) 'The Day-Dream': 'He stoops – to kiss her – on his knee,
"Love, if thy tresses be so dark,
How dark those hidden eyes must be!"'

(xvi) 'The Day-Dream': '... we have slept, my lords.
My beard has grown into my lap.'

6. Tennyson, *Poems*, 1857

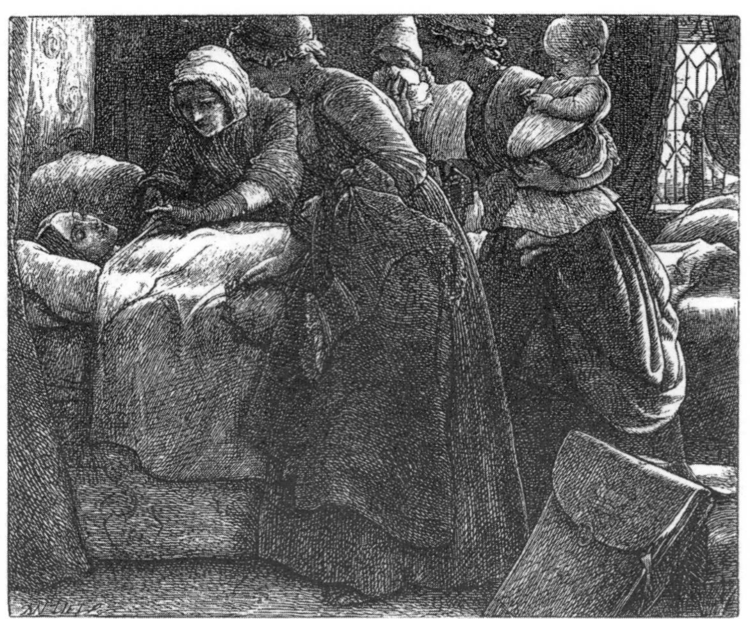

(xvii) 'Edward Gray': 'Sweet Emma Moreland spoke to me:
Bitterly weeping I turn'd away:
Sweet Emma Moreland, love no more
Can touch the heart of Edward Gray.'

(xviii) 'The Lord of Burleigh': 'Then before her time she died.'

7. *The Poets of the Nineteenth Century*, 1857.

(i) 'The Dream': 'He had no breath, no being, but in hers:
She was his voice; he did not speak to her,
But trembled on her words: she was his sight,'

7. *The Poets of the Nineteenth Century*, 1857, *continued.*

(ii) 'Love'*:* 'She half inclosed me with her arms,
She pressed me with a meek embrace;'

8. *Etchings for the Art Union of London by the Etching Club*, 1857.
'The Young Mother', *etching*. Reduced to 88%.

9. *Lays of the Holy Land from Ancient and Modern Poets*, 1858.

'The Finding of Moses':

'And wakes the infant, smiling in his tears, –'

10. *Passages from the Poems of Thomas Hood Illustrated by the Junior Etching Club*, 1858.

(i) 'The Bridge of Sighs', stanza XI, *etching*:

'Where the lamps quiver
So far in the river,
With many a light
From window and casement,
From garret to basement,
She stood, with amazement,
Houseless by night.'

(ii) 'Ruth', stanza IV, *etching*:

'And her hat, with shady brim,
Made her tressy forehead dim ; –
Thus she stood amid the stooks,
Praising God with sweetest looks.'

11. *The Home Affections Pourtrayed by the Poets*, 1858.

(i) 'There's Nae Luck about the House':

> 'For there's nae luck about the house,
> There's nae luck at a';
> There's nae luck about the house,
> When our gudeman's awa'.'

(ii) 'The Border Widow':

'The man lives not I'll love again,
Since that my comely knight is slain;
With one lock of his yellow hair,
I'll bind my heart for evermair.'

12. *John Halifax, Gentleman,* [1861].

'Ursula March', *steel-engraved frontispiece*:

'And there stood the little girl, with a loaf in one hand and a carving knife in the other. She succeeded in cutting off a large slice, and holding it out.'

13. *Nothing New*, [1861].

'Jean Dowglas', *steel-engraved frontispiece*:

'At last she went back to the corner of the cemetery, the spot where Lord Erlistoun had left her. There for many minutes she stood, leaning on the railing, looking across the graves.'

14. *The Valley of a Hundred Fires*, [1861].

'Mrs. Leslie', *steel-engraved frontispiece*:

'... he [John] met Emily coming down-stairs to breakfast, baby crowing in her arms and both looking as blooming and bright as flowers after rain.'

15. *Passages from Modern English Poets Illustrated by the Junior Etching Club*, [1861/2].

'Indolence', *etching*:

'Indolent! Indolent! – Yes, I am indolent:'

16. Anthony Trollope, *Orley Farm*, 1862. Volume 1:
(i) 'Orley Farm'.

(ii) 'Sir Peregrine and his heir'.

Sir Peregrine speaks to young Peregrine Orme on the subject of his university bills:

'Sir Peregrine turned away and walked twice the length of the library; then, returning to the spot where the other stood, he put his hand on his grandson's shoulder. "Well, Peregrine, I will pay them," he said. "I have no doubt that you did so intend when you incurred them; – and that was perhaps natural. I will pay them; but for your own sake, and for your dear mother's sake, I hope that they are not very heavy."'

(iii) 'There was sorrow in her heart, and deep thought in her mind'.

Lady Mason ponders the possibility that legal action may be taken against her:

'There was no smile in her face now, neither was there any tear in her eye. The one and the other emblem were equally alien to her present mood. But there was sorrow at her heart, and deep thought in her mind. She knew that her enemies were conspiring against her, – against her and against her son; and what steps might she best take in order that she might baffle them?'

16. *Orley Farm*, 1862

(iv) 'There is nothing like iron, Sir; nothing'.

Mr Kantwise demonstrates the qualities of his iron furniture in the commercial room of the Bull Inn, Leeds:

'"Nice! I should rather think they are," said Mr. Kantwise, becoming triumphant, – "and for fifteen ten, delivered, boxes included. There's nothing like iron, sir, nothing; you may take my word for that. They're so strong, you know. Look here sir." ... Then lightly poising himself on his toe, he stepped on to the chair, and from thence on to the table. In that position he skilfully brought his feet together, so that his weight was directly on the leg, and gracefully waved his hands over his head.'

(v) 'And then they all marched out of the room, each with his own glass'.

Mr Dockwrath, not wanting to comply with the rules of the commercial room, forces the others to leave:

'And then they all marched out of the room, each with his own glass. Mr. Moulder leading the way with stately step. It was pleasant to see them as they all followed their leader across the open passage of the gateway, in by the bar, and so up the chief staircase.'

(vi) 'Mr. Furnival's welcome home'.

Mr Furnival returns home to find Lucius Mason in the room:

'"How are you, Kitty?" he said to his wife, handing to her the forefinger of his right hand by way of greeting. "Well, Sophy, my love;" and he kissed his daughter. "Oh! Lucius Mason. I am very glad to see you. I can't say I should have remembered you unless I had been told. You are very welcome in Harley Street, and I hope you will often be here."'

(vii) 'Your son Lucius did say – shopping'.

Mrs Furnival meets Lady Mason and is suspicious of her coming to see her husband:

'"I came up on purpose to see Mr. Furnival about some unfortunate law business,' said Lady Mason.
"Oh, indeed! Your son Lucius did say – shopping."
"Yes; I told him so. When a lady is unfortunate enough to be driven to a lawyer for advice, she does not wish to make it known. I should be very sorry if my dear boy were to guess that I had this new trouble; or, indeed, if any one were to know it. I am sure that I shall be as safe with you, dear Mrs. Furnival, as I am with your husband." And she stepped up to the angry matron, looking earnestly into her face.'

(viii) 'Over their wine'.

After dinner at the Cleeve:

'"No more wine for me, sir," said Lucius.
"No wine!" said Sir Peregrine the elder.
"Why, Mason, you'll never get on if that's the way with you," said Peregrine the younger.
"I'll try at any rate," said the other.
"Water-drinker, moody thinker," and Peregerine sang a word or two from an old drinking-song.'

(ix) 'Von Bauhr's Dream'.

The distinguished German lawyer muses on his meeting with the English lawyers and dreams of reform and progress:

'As he sat there, solitary in his bedroom, his hands dropped down by his side, his pipe hung from his mouth on to his breast, and his eyes, turned up to the ceiling, were lighted almost with inspiration ... through his mind and brain, as he sat there wrapped in his old dressing-gown, there ran thoughts which seemed to lift him lightly from the earth into an elysium of justice and mercy.'

(x) 'The English Von Bauhr and his pupil'.

Felix Graham and Augustus Staveley enjoy a brief respite from the law conference in Birmingham:

'The two men had got away from the thickness of the Birmingham smoke, and were seated on the top rung of a gate leading into a stubble field. So far they had gone with mutual consent, but further than this Staveley refused to go. He was seated with a cigar in his mouth. Graham also was smoking, but he was accommodated with a short pipe.'

(xi) 'Christmas at Noningsby. – Morning'.

The walk to the church on Christmas morning; Felix Graham accompanies Madeline Staveley:

'It so fell out, as they started, that Graham found himself walking at Miss Staveley's side, to the great disgust, no doubt, of half a dozen other aspirants for that honour. "I cannot help thinking," he said, as they stepped briskly over the crisp white frost, "that this Christmas-day of ours is a great mistake."'

16. *Orley Farm*, 1862

(xii) 'Christmas at Noningsby. – Evening'.

Blind-man's buff:

'Marian Arbuthnot was not the only soft little laughing darling that wished to be caught, and blinded, so that there was great pulling at the blindman's tails, and much grasping at his outstretched arms before the desired object was attained.'

(xiii) 'Why should I not?'

Sir Peregrine Orme promises to help Lady Mason and realises that he has fallen deeply in love with her:

'"Lady Mason, my house is altogether at your service. If you will be led by me in this matter, you will not leave it till this cloud shall have passed by you. You will be better to be alone now;" and then before she could answer him further, he led her to the door. She felt that it was better for her to be alone, and she hastened up the stairs to her own chamber.

"And why should I not?" said Sir Peregrine to himself, as he again walked the length of the library.'

16. *Orley Farm*, 1862

(xiv) ‘Monkton Grange’.

A general description of the gathering for the hunt which occurs on page 216:

‘And now had arrived a special hunting morning – special, because the meet was in some degree a show meet, appropriate for ladies, at a comfortable distance from Noningsby, and affording a chance of amusement to those who sat in carriages as well as to those on horseback.’

(xv) 'Felix Graham in Trouble'.

Peregrine Orme assists the injured Felix Graham after he has fallen from his horse:

'And then he contrived to picket the horses to two branches, and having got out his case of sherry, poured a small modicum into the silver mug which was attached to the apparatus, and again supported Graham while he drank. "You'll be as right as a trivet by-and-by; only you'll have to make Noningsby your head-quarters for the next six weeks." And then the same idea passed through the mind of each of them; – how little a man need be pitied for such a misfortune if Madeline Staveley would consent to be his nurse.'

(xvi) 'Footsteps in the corridor'.

The scene depicted occurs on page 242, where Madeline Staveley, in attempting to creep past the room where Felix Graham lies unnoticed, encounters the old nurse who has been appointed to care for the young man:

'Mrs. Baker was in the doorway as Madeline attempted to pass by on tiptoe. "Oh, he's a deal better now, Miss Madeline, so that you needn't be afeard of disturbing; – ain't you Mr. Graham?" So she was thus brought into absolute contact with her friend, for the first time since he had hurt himself.'

(xvii) 'The Angel of Light'.

Mary Snow, to whom Felix Graham is technically betrothed, reads a letter from a new admirer:

'"Angel of Light!" it began, "but cold as your own fair name." Poor Mary thought it was very nice and very sweet, and though she was so much afraid of it that she almost wished it away, yet she read it a score of times. Stolen pleasures always are sweet.'

(xviii) 'Lucius Mason in his study'.

Mason at work alone in his room at Orley Farm:

'He had his books before him as he sat there – his Latham and his Pritchard, and he had the jawbone of one savage and the skull of another. His Liverpool bills for unadulterated guano were lying on the table, and a philosophical German treatise on agriculture which he had resolved to study. It became a man, he said to himself, to do a man's work in spite of any sorrow. But, nevertheless, as he sat there, his studies were but of little service to him.'

(xix) 'Peregrine's Eloquence'.

Just after Peregrine Orme has told Lady Mason that he does not wish her to marry Sir Peregrine:

'Peregrine again got up, and standing with his back to the fire, thought over it all again. His soft heart almost relented towards the woman who had borne his rough words with so much patient kindness. Had Sir Peregrine been there then, and could he have condescended so far, he might have won his grandson's consent without much trouble.'

(xx) 'Lady Staveley interrupting her son and Sophia Furnival'.

Lady Staveley bursts in on her son Augustus and the stony-hearted but physically attractive Sophia Furnival to whom he is drawn:

'... Lady Staveley interrupted her son and Sophia Furnival in the back drawing-room, and began to feel that her solicitude for her children would be almost too much for her. Why had she asked that nasty girl to her house, and why would not the nasty girl go away? ... "I can never make a daughter of her if he does marry her," Lady Staveley said to herself, as she looked at them.'

(xxi) 'Lady Mason leaving the court'.

Lady Mason leaves Mr Furnival's chamber:

'And then she went; and as she passed down the dark passage into the new square by the old gate of the Chancellor's court, she met a stout lady .... Lady Mason in her trouble passed the stout lady without taking any notice of her.'

(xxii) 'John Kenneby and Miriam Dockwrath'.

The meeting between John Kenneby and Miriam, with whom he had been in love many years before. Now, long married, she is surrounded by her numerous children:

'And it was opened by Miriam herself. He knew her instantly in spite of all the change. He knew her, but the whole course of his feelings were altered at the moment, and his blood was made to run the other way. And she knew him too. "La, John," she said, "who'd have thought of seeing you?" And she shifted the baby whom she carried from one arm to the other as she gave him her hand in token of welcome.'

(xxiii) ‘Guilty’.

Lady Mason confesses to Sir Peregrine that she is guilty and so cannot marry him:

‘“Sir Peregrine, I am guilty.”
“Guilty! Guilty of what?” he said, startled rather than instructed by her words.
“Guilty of all this with which they charge me.” And then she threw herself at his feet, and wound her arms round his knees.’

(xxiv) 'Lady Mason after her Confession'.

Lady Mason ponders on her confession of guilt in the private isolation of her own room:

'But soon the bitter air pierced her through and through, and she shivered with the cold as she sat there. After a while she got herself a shawl, wrapped it close around her, and then sat down again. She bethought herself that she might have to remain in this way for hours, so she rose again and locked the door.'

(xxv) ‘Bread Sauce is so ticklish’.

Felix Graham’s nurse, Mrs Baker addresses him:

‘“Bread sauce is so ticklish; a simmer too much and it’s clean done for,” Mrs. Baker said with a voice of great solicitude. But she had been accustomed perhaps to patients whose appetites were fastidious. The pheasant and the bread sauce and the mashed potatoes, all prepared by Mrs. Baker’s own hands to be eaten as spoon meat, disappeared with great celerity; and then, as Graham sat sipping the solitary glass of sherry that was allowed to him, meditating that he would begin his letter the moment the glass was empty, Augustus Staveley again made his appearance.’

(xxvi) 'Never is a very long word'.

Lady Staveley and her daughter discuss the hopeless case Peregrine Orme has in pressing his suit with her:

'"But why should you be so certain about it, my love? He does not intend to trouble you with his suit, – nor do I. Why not leave that to time? There can be no reason why you should not see him again on a friendly footing when this embarrassment between you shall have passed away."
"There would be no reason, mamma, if he were quite sure that there could never be any other footing."
"Never is a very long word."'

(xxvii) '"Tom" she said, "I have come back"'.

Mrs Furnival's return home having tried to see Lady Mason, whom she suspects of having an affair with her husband. Having walked out on him and moved into lodgings nearby, she now has been assured by Mrs Orme that she is mistaken:

'"Tom," she said, going up to him, and speaking in a low voice, "I have come back again." And she stood before him as a suppliant.'

(xxviii) 'Lady Mason going before the Magistrates'.

The scene is barely described by Trollope. Millais notes carefully, however, that Lady Mason's face '... was covered by a deep veil.'

(xxix) 'Sir Peregrine at Mr. Round's Office'.

Sir Peregrine attempts to plead his lover's case with the solicitor acting for the accuser of Lady Mason, Mr Mason of Groby Park:

'There was much ceremonial talk between them before Sir Peregrine could bring himself to declare the purport which had brought him there. Mr. Round of course protested that he was very sorry for all this affair. The case was not in his hands personally. He had hoped many years since that the matter was closed. His client, Mr. Mason of Groby Park, had insisted that it should be reopened; and now he, Mr. Round, really hardly knew what to say about it.
"But, Mr. Round, do you think it is quite impossible that the trial should even now be abandoned?" asked Sir Peregrine very carefully.'

(xxx) 'Tell me, Madelaine, are you happy now?'

On a walk Madeline Staveley speaks to her father about her love for Felix Graham ('Madelaine' on the plate but 'Madeline' in the text):

'But just before they came out again upon the road, her father stopped her and asked a direct question. "Tell me, Madeline, are you happy now?"
"Yes, papa."
"That is right. And what you are to understand is this; Mr. Graham will now be privileged by your mother and me to address you. He has already asked my permission to do so, and I told him that I must consider the matter before I either gave it or withheld it. I shall now give him that permission." Whereupon Madeline made her answer by a slight pressure upon his arm.'

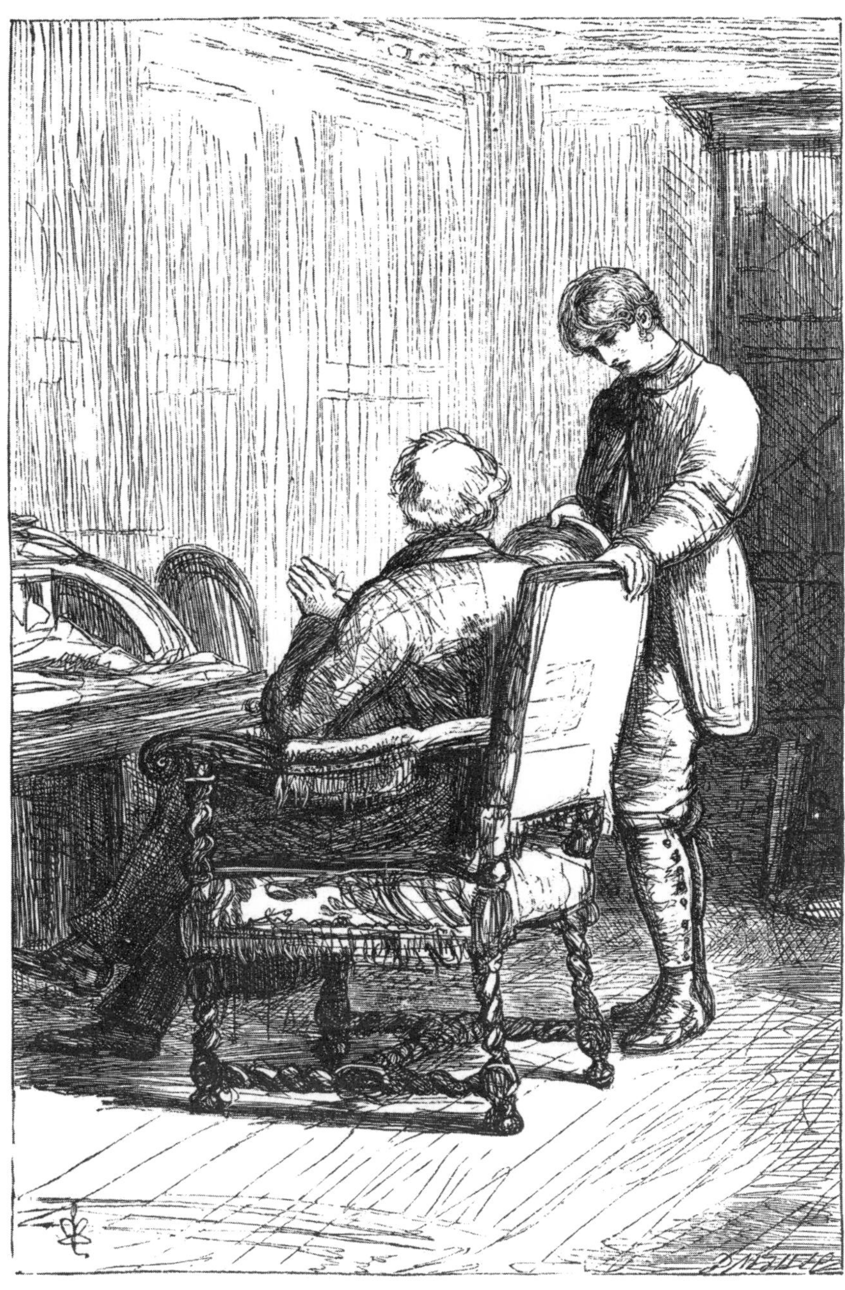

(xxxi) 'No surrender'.

Sir Peregrine Orme and his grandson. Sir Peregrine has just made the announcement that he is to hand over The Cleeve to the young man at Lady-day. Young Peregrine speaks.

'"But what I say is this: you should never give up as long as you live. There's a sort of feeling about it which I can't explain. One should always say to oneself, No surrender." And Peregrine, as he spoke, stood up from his chair, thrust his hands into his trousers-pockets, and shook his head.'

(xxxii) 'Mr. Chaffanbrass and Mr. Solomon Aram'.

The two lawyers who will act for Lady Mason discuss the case:

'The room in which Mr. Aram was now sitting was furnished with much more attention to comfort than is usual in lawyers' chambers. Mr. Chaffanbrass was at present lying, with his feet up, on a sofa against the wall, in a position of comfort never attained by him elsewhere till the after-dinner hours had come to him; and Mr. Aram himself filled an easy lounging-chair.'

(xxxiii) 'The Court'.

The scene in the court-room.

'As she thus looked her gaze fell on one face that she had not seen for years, and their eyes met. It was the face of Joseph Mason of Groby, who sat opposite to her; and as she looked at him her own countenance did not quail for a moment. Her own countenance did not quail; but his eyes fell gradually down, and when he raised them again she had averted her face.'

(xxxiv) 'The Drawing-room at Noningsby'.

Felix Graham sits talking to Madeline while Lady Staveley dozes next to them:

'She did sleep, and Felix was left alone with his love.

And yet he was not altogether alone. He could not say to her those words which he was now bound to say; which he longed to say in order that he might know whether the next stage of his life was to be light or dark.'

(xxxv) 'And how are they all at Noningsby?'

Just after Sophia Furnival has written a cold letter to Lucius Mason in which she says: '… marriage is a very serious thing, and there is so much to be considered!'

'But the last letter was not written throughout without interruption. She was just declaring how on her part she hoped that her present uncertain tenure of her lover's hand might at some future time become certain, when Augustus Staveley was announced. Sophia, who was alone in the drawing-room, rose from her table, gracefully, slipped her note under the cover of the desk, and courteously greeted her visitor. "And how are they all at dear Noningsby?" she asked.'

(xxxvi) 'How can I bear it?'

A distraught Lady Mason reveals her misery to her friend Mrs Orme:

'"Do you know I was thinking to-day that my mind would fail me, and that I should be mad before this is over? How can I bear it? how can I bear it?" And rising from her seat, she walked rapidly through the room, holding back her hair from her brows with both her hands.'

(xxxvii) 'Bridget Bolster in Court'.

The witness for the prosecution awaits the onslaught from Mr Chaffanbrass.

'Then Mr. Chaffanbrass rose from his seat, and every one knew that his work was cut out for him.... It was now necessary to demolish Bridget Bolster, and the opinion was general that if anybody could do it Mr. Chaffanbrass was the man ...
"I think you say you're – a chambermaid?" That was the first question which Chaffanbrass asked, and Bridget Bolster gave a little start as she heard his sharp, angry, disagreeable voice.'

(xxxviii) 'Lucius Mason, as he leaned on the gate that was no longer his own'.

Lucius Mason knows his mother's guilt, even though she has walked free from the court. He has no other choice than to return his home, Orley Farm, to its rightful owner, Joseph Mason of Groby Park:

'It had been his constant practice to walk up and down from his own hall door to his own gate on the high-road, perhaps comforting himself too warmly with the reflection that the ground on which he walked was all his own. He had no such comfort now, as he made his way down the accustomed path and leaned upon the gate, thinking over what he had heard.'

(xxxix) 'Farewell!'

Mrs Orme bids farewell to Lady Mason:

'"No, no; of course you must go. Oh, my darling, oh, my friend," and she threw herself into the other's arms.'

(xl) 'Farewell'.

Sir Peregrine and the disgraced Lady Mason part. Note that in some later copies of the book, such as the reprint of 1866, this final plate is omitted.

'"May God bless you, Mary, and preserve you, and give back to you the comforts of a quiet spirit, and a heart at rest! Till you hear that I am under the ground you will know that there is one living who loves you well." Then he took her in his arms, twice kissed her on the forehead, and left the room without further speech on either side.'

17. Dinah Mulock (Mrs Craik), *Mistress and Maid*, [1862].

'Mistress and Maid', page 48 (Hilary is the mistress and Elizabeth the maid), *steel-engraved frontispiece*:

'And Hilary tried to contemplate gravely the scrawled and blotted page, which looked very much as if a large spider had walked into the ink-bottle and then walked out again on a tour of investigation.'

18. Anne Isabella Robertson, *Myself and my Relatives*, 1863.

'Myself and my Relatives', *steel-engraved frontispiece*:

The narrator of the novel, Jessie Keppleton, is staying in a farmhouse where a fire breaks out at night. In the panic to escape a baby is left behind in the nursery. A young servant girl, Maggy Bond, makes a valiant and successful rescue but dies herself in the inferno.

'"Put the ladder to the casement, John," shouted a clear intrepid voice, and in the next instant I beheld a figure fleeing towards the burning house. It vanished quickly, while a roar burst from the spectators. It was Maggy Bond that had disappeared within the fearful mass of smoke and fire! I stood immoveably looking on at the lurid glare colouring the very sky above, feeling almost paralysed with terror. Every one seemed watching the house breathlessly.

"She's lost! She's lost!" shouted out half a dozen voices in a breath. Now the little casement opens, the fire has not touched the nursery yet; and as John ascends the ladder towards it, out come two red arms, bearing the baby in his night-dress, still half asleep. John catches him tightly, and puts him under one arm, while he cautiously descends the ladder, step by step.'

19. Sarah Tytler (Henrietta Keddie), *Papers for Thoughtful Girls*, 1863.

(i) 'Cis Berry's Arrival'.

'A stranger stood on the discoloured doorstep; a woman, a girl, a little, brown, warm-cheeked girl, with a little hat on her erect head ...'

(ii) 'Our Sister Grizel' to 'Youth'.

'How pretty it was to see Grizel in the flaxen-haired, bright-cheeked fairness and bloom of her twelve or thirteen summers, holding the year-old child, coaxing it to open its cherry of a mouth ...'

(iii) 'Dame Dorothy' to 'Friendship'.

'She [Miss Lavinia the school-teacher] called Miss Anne Baldwin and Miss Dorothy Fenton to stand before her chair.'

(iv) To 'Kindliness', the section called 'Nürnberg Eggs'. The design is entitled 'Herr Willy Koenig'.

'He was an ardent, vivacious fellow, with a quick perception of the ludicrous;'

23. W. Wilkie Collins, *No Name*, [1863/4].

'No Name – One half-hour', *steel-engraved frontispiece*:

'For one half-hour to come, she determined to wait there, and count the vessels as they went by. If, in that time, an even number passed her – the sign given, should be a sign to live. If the uneven number prevailed – the end should be Death.'

20. *Wordsworth's Poems for the Young*, 1863.

Title-page vignette of a little girl reading intently.

24. Victor Hugo, *Les Misérables*, [1864].

'Cosette', *steel-engraved frontispiece*:

'This is what she read: - The reduction of the Universe to a single being, the dilation of a single being as far as GOD, such is love.

Love is the salutation of the angels to the stars.'

25. [J. E. Millais], *The Parables of Our Lord and Saviour Jesus Christ*, 1864.

(i) 'The Sower'.

'Behold, a sower went forth to sow;

And when he sowed, some seeds fell by the way side, and the fowls came and devoured them up:'

(ii) 'The Leaven'.

'The kingdom of heaven is like unto leaven, which a woman took, and hid in three measures of meal, *till the whole was leavened*.'

(iii) ‘The Tares’.

‘The kingdom of heaven is likened unto a man which sowed good seed in his field:

But while men slept, his enemy came and sowed tares among the wheat, and went his way.’

25. *The Parables*, 1864

(iv) 'The Hidden Treasure'.

'The kingdom of heaven is like unto treasure hid in a field; the which when a man hath found, he hideth, and for joy thereof goeth and selleth all that he hath, and buyeth that field.'

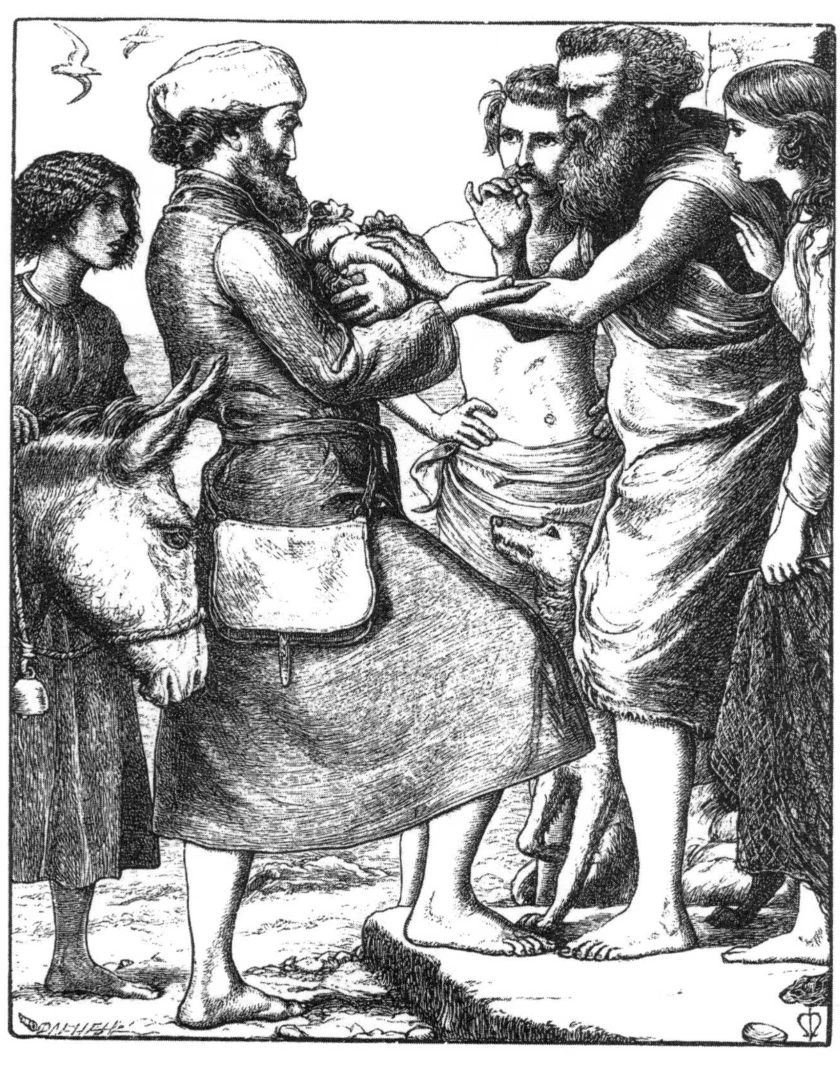

(v) 'The Pearl of Great Price'.

'The kingdom of heaven is like unto a merchant man, seeking goodly pearls: Who, when he had found one pearl of great price, went and sold all that he had, and bought it.'

25. *The Parables*, 1864

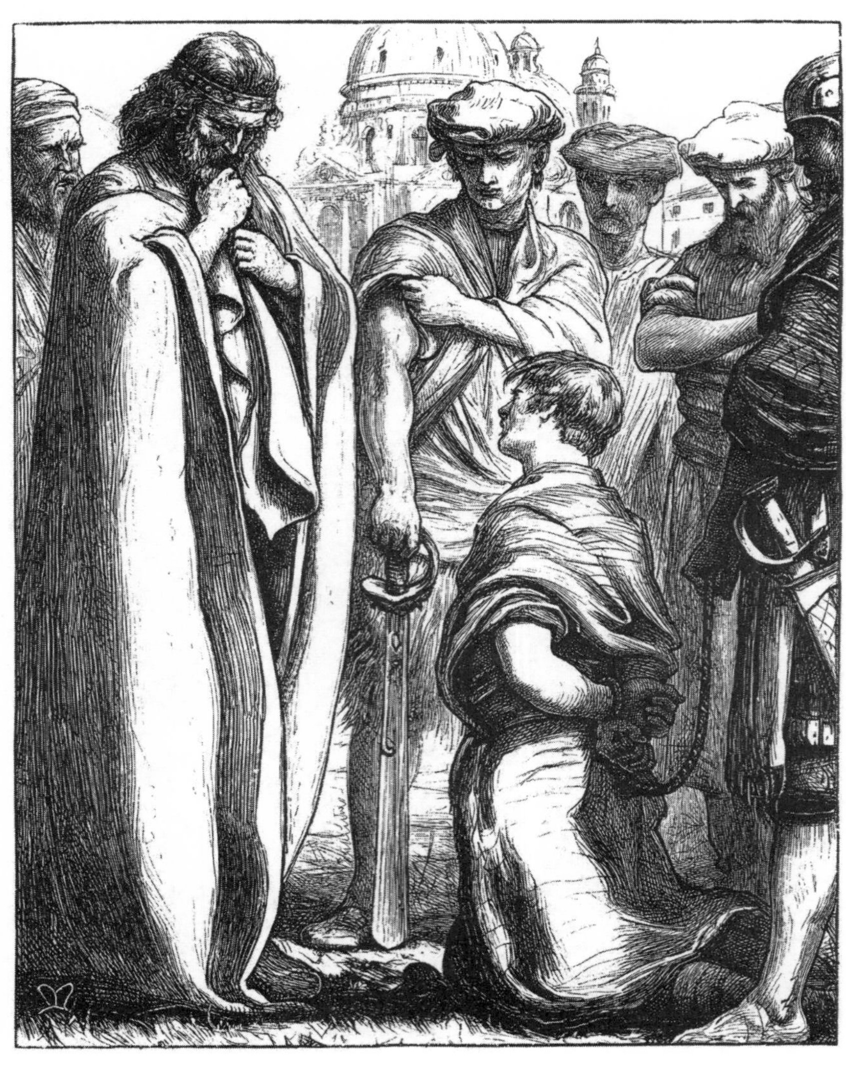

(vi) 'The Unmerciful Servant'.

'The servant therefore fell down, and worshipped him, saying, Lord, have patience with me, and I will pay thee all.

Then the lord of that servant was moved with compassion, and loosed him, and forgave him the debt.'

The servant goes away and does not show similar compassion to his debtor:

'Then his lord, after that he had called him, said unto him, O thou wicked servant, I forgave thee all that debt, because thou desiredst me:

Shouldest not thou also have had compassion on thy fellow servant, even as I had pity on thee?

And his lord was wroth, and delivered him to the tormentors, till he should pay all that was due unto him.'

(vii) ‘The Labourers in the Vineyard’.

‘But he answered one of them, and said, Friend, I do thee no wrong: didst not thou agree with me for a penny?

Take that thine is, and go thy way: I will give unto this last, even as unto thee.

Is it not lawful for me to do what I will with mine own? Is thine eye evil, because I am good?

So the last shall be first, and the first last: for many be called, but few chosen.’

25. *The Parables*, 1864

(viii) 'The Wicked Husbandmen'.

'But when the husbandmen saw the son, they said among themselves, This is the heir; come, let us kill him, and let us seize on his inheritance.

And they caught him, and cast him out of the vineyard, and slew him....

Jesus saith unto them, Did ye never read in the Scriptures, the stone which the builders rejected, the same is become the head of the corner: this is the Lord's doing, and it is marvellous in our eyes?

Therefore say I unto you, The kingdom of God shall be taken from you, and given to a nation bringing forth the fruits thereof.

And whosoever shall fall on this stone shall be broken: but on whomsoever it shall fall, it will grind him to powder.'

(ix) 'The Wise and Foolish Virgins'.

'Then shall the kingdom of heaven be likened unto ten virgins, which took their lamps, and went forth to meet the bridegroom. And five of them were wise, and five were foolish. They that were foolish took their lamps, and took no oil with them: But the wise took oil in their vessels with their lamps. While the bridegroom tarried, they all slumbered and slept.

And at midnight there was a cry made, Behold, the bridegroom cometh; go ye out to meet him. Then all those virgins arose, and trimmed their lamps. And the foolish said unto the wise, Give us of your oil; for our lamps are gone out.

But the wise answered, saying, Not so; lest there be not enough for us and you: but go ye rather to them that sell, and buy for yourselves.'

25. *The Parables*, 1864

(x) 'The Foolish Virgins'.

'And while they went to buy, the bridegroom came; and they that were ready went in with him to the marriage: and the door was shut.

Afterward came also the other virgins, saying, Lord, Lord, open to us.

But he answered and said, Verily I say unto you, I know you not.

Watch therefore, for ye know neither the day nor the hour wherein the Son of man cometh.'

(xi) 'The Good Samaritan'.

'A certain man went down from Jerusalem to Jericho, and fell among thieves, which stripped him of his raiment, and wounded him, and departed, leaving him half dead....

But a certain Samaritan, as he journeyed, came where he was: and when he saw him, he had compassion on him, And went to him, and bound up his wounds, pouring in oil and wine, and set him on his own beast, and brought him to an inn, and took care of him.'

25. *The Parables*, 1864

(xii) 'The Importunate Friend'.

'And I say unto you, Ask, and it shall be given you; seek, and ye shall find; knock, and it shall be opened unto you.

For every one that asketh receiveth, and he that seeketh findeth; and to him that knocketh it shall be opened.

If a son shall ask bread of any of you that is a father, will he give him a stone? or if he ask a fish, will he for a fish give him a serpent?'

(xiii) 'The Marriage Feast'.

This design actually accompanies 'The Parable of the Marriage of the King's Son'. (For a detailed discussion of the confusion over this Parable see Lutyens (1975) pp.xiv–xv.):

'And when the king came in to see the guests, he saw there a man which had not on a wedding garment:

And he saith unto him, Friend, how camest thou in hither not having a wedding garment? And he was speechless.

Then said the king to the servants, Bind him hand and foot, and take him away, and cast him into outer darkness; there shall be weeping and gnashing of teeth.

For many are called, but few are chosen.'

(xiv) ‘The Lost Sheep’.

‘What man of you, having an hundred sheep, if he lose one of them, doth not leave the ninety and nine in the wilderness, and go after that which is lost, until he find it?

And when he hath found it, he layeth it on his shoulders, rejoicing.’

(xv) 'The Lost Piece of Silver'.

'Either what woman having ten pieces of silver, if she lose one piece, doth not light a candle, and sweep the house, and seek diligently till she find it?

And when she hath found it, she calleth her friends and her neighbours together, saying, Rejoice with me; for I have found the piece which I had lost.

Likewise, I say unto you, there is joy in the presence of the angels of God over one sinner that repenteth.'

(xvi) 'The Prodigal Son'.

'And he arose, and came to his father. But when he was yet a great way off, his father saw him, and had compassion, and ran, and fell on his neck, and kissed him.'

(xvii) 'The Rich Man and Lazarus'.

'There was a certain rich man, which was clothed in purple and fine linen, and fared sumptuously every day:

And there was a certain beggar named Lazarus, which was laid at his gate, full of sores,

And desiring to be fed with the crumbs which fell from the rich man's table: moreover the dogs came and licked his sores.'

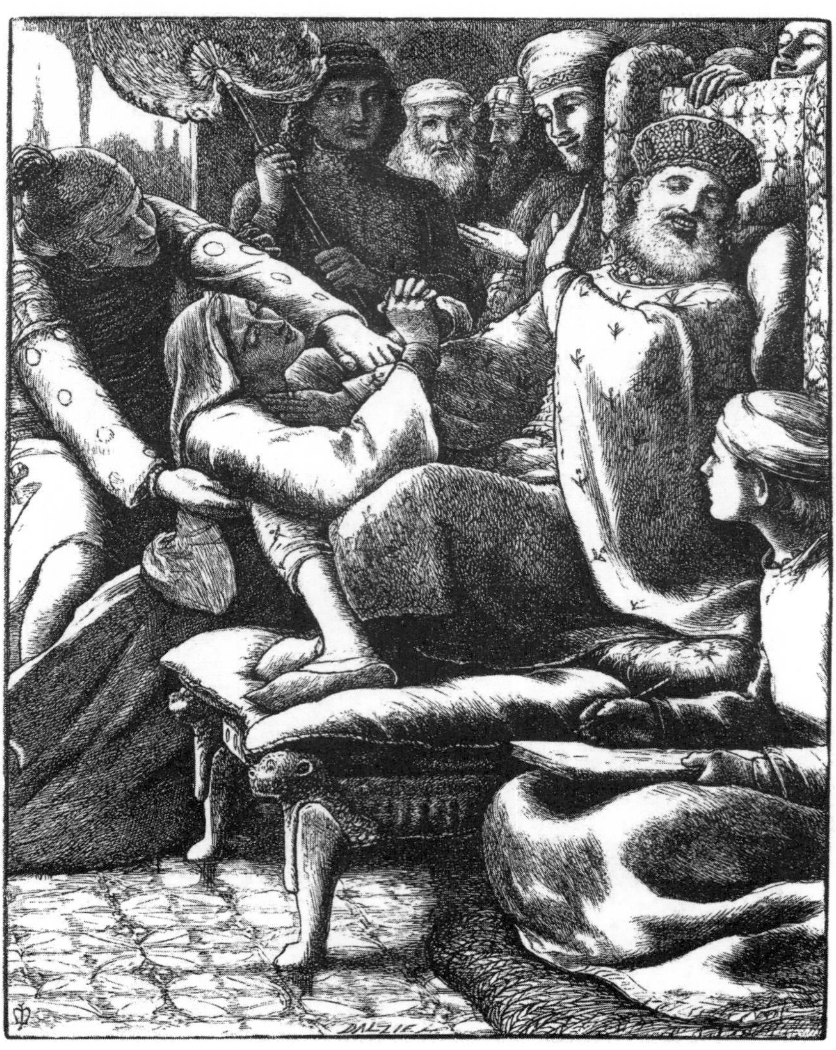

(xviii) 'The Unjust Judge'.

'There was in a city a judge, which feared not God, neither regarded man:

And there was widow in that city; and she came unto him, saying, Avenge me of mine adversary.

And he would not for awhile: but afterward he said within himself, Though I fear not God, nor regard man;

Yet because this widow troubleth me, I will avenge her, lest by her continual coming she weary me.'

(xix) ‘The Pharisee and the Publican’.

‘Two men went up into the temple to pray; the one a Pharisee, and the other a Publican.

The Pharisee stood and prayed thus with himself, God, I thank thee, that I am not as other men are, extortioners, unjust, adulterers, or even as this Publican.

I fast twice in the week, I give tithes of all that I possess.

And the Publican, standing afar off, would not lift up so much as his eyes unto heaven, but smote upon his breast, saying, God be merciful to me a sinner.

I tell you, this man went down to his house justified rather than the other:

For every one that exalteth himself shall be abased; and he that humbleth himself shall be exalted.’

(xx) ‘The Good Shepherd’.

‘I am the good shepherd: the good shepherd giveth his life for the sheep.’

26. Caroline Elizabeth Sarah Norton (later Stirling-Maxwell), *Lost and Saved*, [1864].

'Lost and Saved', *steel-engraved frontispiece*:

'Beatrice Brooke was a beautiful a woman as could be seen or imagined ... She found Frank peevish, sick and suffering ... She laid him in her bosom, she caressed and fondled him, she spoke the sweet unmeaning words which are mother's music to young children ... At length it came, that blessing of slumber.'

27. Anthony Trollope, *Rachel Ray*, 1864.

Steel-engraved frontispiece. No reference to a particular point in the text identified; it is likely to depict Rachel at the stile where Luke Rowan remarks on the scene, although he is not shown by Millais (page 33):

'"Rachel," said he, after they had remained there in silence for a moment, "live as long as you may, never on God's earth will you look on any sight more lovely than that. Ah! do you see the man's arm, as it were; the deep purple cloud, like a huge hand stretched out from some other world to take you? Do you see it?"'

28. Anthony Trollope, *The Small House at Allington*, 1864.
(i) 'The Croquet Match'.

29. *Dalziel's Illustrated Arabian Nights Entertainments*, 1865.

(i) 'Zobeidè discovers the young man reading the Koran', from 'The History of Zobeidè'. March 1864.

'I perceived, also, a small carpet, spread out in the same manner as those which we are accustomed to kneel upon when we pray. A young man, of a pleasant countenance, was seated upon this carpet, reading aloud, with great attention, from the Koran, which lay before him on a small desk. Astonished and delighted at this sight, I endeavoured to account to myself for the astonishing fact that he was the only person alive in a town where everyone else was petrified, and I felt sure that there was something very extraordinary in this.'

(ii) 'Aminè and the Lady', from 'The History of Aminè'. March 1864.

'My guide conducted me through a court into a large hall, where I was received by a young lady of incomparable beauty. She immediately came towards me; and, after embracing me, she made me sit next to her on a sofa, over which there was a sort of throne, or canopy, formed of precious wood enriched with diamonds.'

31. J. Bertrand Payne, *The Lineage and Pedigree of the Family of Millais*, 1865

The family coat of arms including shield, helmet, etc., *etching*.

Burke's *Peerage, Baronetage and Knightage* (10th edn, 1970) gives the following description of the Millais Arms, Crest and Motto:

'Arms – Per bend sinister or and az. An estoile of eight points between three fleurs-de-lis, two in fesse and one in base countered changed. Crest – In front of a dexter hand gauntleted and couped gu. and estoile of eight points or. Motto – Ars Longa, vita brevis.'

32. Henry Leslie, *Little Songs for Me to Sing*, 1865.

(i) Untitled frontispiece.

(ii) 'Twinkle, Twinkle, Little Star'.

(iii) 'Little Brother Charlie'.

(iv) 'God's Works'.

(v) 'Mary's Little Lamb'.

(vi) 'The Sweet Story of Old'.

(vii) 'Morning and Evening Hymns'.

32. *Little Songs for Me to Sing*, 1865

33. *A Selection of Etchings by the Etching Club*, 1865.
'Happy Springtime', *etching*.

34. Frederick Locker, *A Selection from the Work of Frederick Locker*, 1865.

Portrait of Locker, *etched frontispiece*.

35. Eliza Tabor (Stephenson), [1865]. *See overleaf.*

36. Daniel Defoe, *Robinson Crusoe*, 1866.

Steel-engraved title-page design:

Crusoe reading with his dog at his feet and his cat at his elbow.

35. Eliza Tabor (Stephenson), *St. Olave's*, [1865].

'Alice'. Alice Grey arranges flowers, *steel-engraved frontispiece*:

'With practised skill, such as no artist could have taught her, she blended and contrasted the tints, and placed each leaf in its natural fall. Every now and then she would bend her pretty head on one side, to take in the general effect, then make some little alteration in the arrangement.'

37. [Jean Ingelow], *Studies for Stories from Girls' Lives*, 1866.

(i) 'The Cumberers.'

'I persuaded her to lie down, while I went and sat on the stairs.'

(ii) 'The Stolen Treasure.'

'The merry little face peeped out over her shoulder for she was carrying little Mary pickapack.'

38. *Millais's Collected Illustrations*, 1866.

Title-page design.

43. Johann Wolfgang von Goethe, *Egmont*, 1868.

'He falls asleep. Music accompanies his sleep ... a bright vision appears. Freedom, draped like an angel, with a halo rests upon a cloud ... she seems to pity him.'

44. H. Cholmondeley Pennell, *Puck on Pegasus*, 1869.

'Fire': 'The Engines, Ho – back for your lives! –
The swarthy helmets gleam:
Flash fast, broad wheel,
Hold, wood and steel, ... '

46. Henry Leslie, *Henry Leslie's Musical Annual*, 1871.

'A Reverie' or 'Girl at the Window', *steel-engraved frontispiece.*

46. *Musical Annual*, 1871

49. *Etchings for the Art Union of London by the Etching Club*, 1872.
(ii) 'The Baby House', *etching*.

(i) ‘Going to the Park’, *etching*.

52. Samuel Carter Hall, *An Old Story: A Temperance Tale*, [1875] .

Although no particular text is illustrated, the image is clearly of a woman waiting sorrowfully and anxiously for the return of her alcoholic husband.

57. William Makepeace Thackeray, *The Memoirs of Barry Lyndon, Esq. ... and The Fatal Boots*, 1879 .

(i) 'A Rhyme for Aristotle':

'"Doctor," says I, looking waggishly at him, "do you know ever a rhyme for *Aristotle*?"
"Port, if you plaise," says Mr. Goldsmith, laughing. And we had *six rhymes for Aristotle* before we left the coffee-house that evening.'

(ii) 'Barry Lyndon's First Love':

'In the course of our diversion Nora managed to scratch her arm, and it bled, and she screamed, and it was mighty round and white, and I tied it up, and I believe was permitted to kiss her hand;'

57. *The Memoirs of Barry Lyndon, Esq.*, 1879

(iii) 'The Intercepted Letters':

'My Lady Lyndon's letters were none the worse for being opened, and a great deal the better;'

(iv) 'The Last Days of Barry Lyndon'.

Barry Lyndon's mother sits with him in the Fleet Prison:

'She is very old, and is sitting by my side at this moment in the prison, working: ... we manage to eke out a miserable existence, quite unworthy of the famous and fashionable Barry Lyndon.'

57. *The Memoirs of Barry Lyndon, Esq.*, 1879

58. *By the Etching Club*, 1879.
'A Penny for her Thoughts', *etching,* reduced to 75%.

63. Henry Leslie, *Leslie's Songs for Little Folks*, [1883].

A nun gazing out of her convent window.

'St. Agnes' Eve': 'Deep on the convent-roof the snows
Are sparkling to the moon:
My breath to heaven like vapour goes:
May my soul follow soon!'

68. John Guille Millais, *A Breath from the Veldt*, 1895.

'The Last Trek', *electro-etched frontispiece*, reduced from 149 × 220 mm (5⅞ × 8⅝ in).

67. John Guille Millais, *Game Birds and Shooting Sketches ...*, 1892.

An *autotype reproduction* of a drawing of Thomas Bewick printed in brown, reduced from 250 x 178 mm (9⅞ × 7 in). The artist seated holding a portfolio with stuffed birds on the table and at his feet. Geoffroy Millais has pointed out that Millais has placed Bewick in the sitter's chair in his studio. Both this and the table were in the artist's last home, 2 Palace Gate, Kensington, and remain with the family today.

69. John Guille Millais, *The Wildfowler in Scotland*, 1901.

'The Morning Flight', *photogravure frontispiece*, reduced from 214 × 147 mm (8⅜ × 5¾ in).

70. Wace, *Ses Oeuvres.*

Apparently for a projected work by John Sullivan of Jersey. The book does not appear to have reached publication.

PLATES

The Periodical Illustrations

1. THE ARGOSY [Pp6004 gs]

(i) 'The Sighing of the Shell', June 1866. Poem by George MacDonald:

'It whispers of love – 'tis a prophet-shell –
Of a peace that comes, and all shall be well;
It speaks not a word of your love to me,
But it tells me to love you eternally.'

2. THE MAGAZINE OF ART [Pp1931 pci]

(ii) Facing page 54 in the latter section of the magazine of 1878 is a further engraving by Swain after a painting by Millais: 'The North-West Passage' or 'It might be done and England ought to do it'.

(i) 'The Fair Maidens', 1878

Frontispiece, with an accompanying note about the artist: 'Unconventionality of composition, with little fear of unfilled spaces and still less of repetitions of attitude or action, is one of the main characteristics of his drawings', and continuing that the drawing 'has, among its other beauties, the fresh feeling of work done from life', and that 'it gives pleasant evidence that the hand of the artist has not, in this or any other range of his art, forgotten its old cunning'.

3. THE CHURCHMAN'S FAMILY MAGAZINE [Pp357 b]

To 'The New Curate'.

(i) 'Let that be, please!', January 1863.

(ii) 'You will forgive me, won't you?', February 1863.

4. THE CORNHILL MAGAZINE [Pp 6004 gk]

(i) 'Unspoken Dialogue', February 1860. Poem by R. Monckton Milnes:

'Dear child! he comes. – Nay, blush not so
To have your secret known:
'Tis best, 'tis best, that I should go –
And leave you here alone.'

(ii) 'Lord Lufton and Lucy Robarts', April 1860. To Anthony Trollope, *Framley Parsonage*.

The scene depicted occurs on page 459 and shows the first meeting between Lucy Robarts and Lord Lufton:

'Now we may say she was fairly caught, and Lord Lufton, taking a pair of pheasants from the gamekeeper, and swinging them over his shoulder, walked off with his prey.'

(iii) 'Was it not a lie?', June 1860, facing page 691. To Anthony Trollope, *Framley Parsonage*.

The scene depicted occurs on page 700 immediately after Lucy Robarts has rejected Lord Lufton's proposal. She was unable to speak the truth of her feelings:

'And when he was well gone – absolutely out of sight from the window – Lucy walked steadily up to her room, locked the door, and then threw herself on the bed. Why – oh! why had she told such a falsehood? Could anything justify her in a lie? Was it not a lie – knowing as she did that she loved him with all her loving heart?'

(iv) 'The Crawley Family', August 1860, facing page 129. To Anthony Trollope, *Framley Parsonage.*

The opening lines of chapter 22, 'Hogglestock Parsonage' are described:

'At the end of the last chapter, we left Lucy Robarts waiting for an introduction to Mrs. Crawley, who was sitting with one baby in her lap while she was rocking another who lay in a cradle at her feet. Mr. Crawley, in the meanwhile, had risen from his seat with his finger between the leaves of an old grammar out of which he had been teaching his two elder children. The whole Crawley family was thus before them when Mrs. Robarts and Lucy entered the sitting-room.'

(v) 'Lady Lufton and the Duke of Omnium', October 1860, facing page 462. To Anthony Trollope, *Framley Parsonage*.

The scene depicted occurs on page 473 and shows the tense meeting between Lady Lufton and the Duke of Omnium at Miss Dunstable's party:

'... she curtseyed low and slowly, and with a haughty arrangement of her drapery that was all her own; but the curtsey, though it was eloquent, did not say half so much, – did not reprobate the habitual iniquities of the duke with a voice nearly as potent, as that which was expressed in the gradual fall of her eye and the gradual pressure of her lips.'

(vi) 'Last Words', November 1860, facing page 513. Poem by Owen Meredith which opens with these lines:

'Will, are you sitting and watching there yet? And I know, by a certain skill
That grows out of utter wakefulness, the night must be far spent,Will:'

The poem continues some lines later:

'For woman, Will, is a thorny flower: it breaks, and we bleed and smart:
The blossom falls at the fairest, and the thorn runs into the heart.'

(vii) 'Mrs. Gresham and Miss Dunstable', January 1861, facing page 48. To Anthony Trollope, *Framley Parsonage*.

The scene depicted occurs on page 60, where the two women discuss affairs of the heart:

'"I do lack courage. That's just it," said Mrs. Gresham, still giving a twist here and a set there to some of the small sprigs which constituted the background of her bouquet.'

(viii) 'Temptation', February 1861, facing page 229. To 'Horace Saltoun'.

The story opens:

'It is now many a long year since I and Horace Saltoun found ourselves extended one fine summer's day on a luxuriously mossy bank that overlooked one of the loveliest dales of the north-west of England.... So while we smoked our short pipes we philosophized after our crude fashion, pitied the fellows who had been "spun," as the phrase goes, and pronounced dogmatically enough on the merits of the case.'

(ix) '"Mark," she said, "the men are here"', March 1861, facing page 342. To Anthony Trollope, *Framley Parsonage*.

The scene depicted occurs on page 352, where Fanny Robarts tells her husband that the bailiffs are at the door intent on reclaiming Framley Parsonage:

'"Mark," she said, "The men are here; they are in the yard". "I know it", he answered gruffly.'

(x) 'Irené', April 1862, facing page 478. To 'Irené'. The poem is signed 'RM'.

> 'Irené hears, for every spirit breath
> That flits abroad is by Irené hearkened;
> And, reverent, she has knelt as mute as death
> Beside the window since her chamber darkened.'

(xi) 'The Bishop and the Knight', July 1862, facing page 100. The poem is signed 'M'.

'Low at the Bishop's feet he knelt,
His black locks thickly sown with gray,
As though the sorrows he had felt
Had stolen half his youth away:
His careworn features did express
A dying hope – a long distress –
An unknown depth of lowliness.'

(xii) 'Please Ma'am, can we have the peas to shell?', September 1862, facing page 364 with an initial letter design on page 364. To Anthony Trollope, *The Small House at Allington.*

The scene depicted occurs on page 382 where Mrs Dale, pondering what Lily has just said to her, is interrupted by the maid:

'"Mamma will stay at home to eat the peas."

And then she repeated to herself the words which Lily had spoken, sitting there, leaning with her elbow on her knee, and her head upon her hand.

"Please, ma'am, cook says, can we have the peas to shell?" and then her reverie was broken.'

Initial letters to the chapter openings facing xii and xiii.

(xiii) '"And you love me!" said she', October 1862, facing page 552 with an initial letter design on page 552. To Anthony Trollope, *The Small House at Allington*.

The scene depicted occurs on page 563, where Johnny Eames makes a declaration of love to Amelia Roper, even though he is really in love with Lily Dale:

'"And you love me?" said she.
"Of course I love you." And then, upon hearing these words, Amelia threw herself into his arms.'

(xiv) 'It's all the fault of the naughty Birds', November 1862, facing page 663 with an initial letter design on page 663. To Anthony Trollope, *The Small House at Allington*.

The scene depicted occurs on page 667 after the unsuccessful shoot. The men Lily is referring to are her lover, Adolphus Crosbie, and her sister Bell's lover, her cousin, Bernard:

'"Uncle," said Lily, "these men have shot nothing, and you cannot conceive how unhappy they are in consequence. It's all the fault of the naughty partridges."'

Initial letters to the chapter openings facing xiv and xv.

(xv) '"Mr. Cradell, your hand," said Lupex', December 1862, facing page 780 with an initial letter design on page 780. To Anthony Trollope, *The Small House at Allington.*

The scene depicted occurs on page 786. It shows the confrontation between Mr Cradell and Mr and Mrs Lupex:

'"Mr. Cradell, your hand," said Lupex, who had advanced as far as the second glass of brandy-and-water, but had not been allowed to go beyond it. "There has been a misunderstanding between us; let it be forgotten."'

(xvi) 'Why, it's young Eames', January 1863, facing page 56 with an initial letter design on page 56. To Anthony Trollope, *The Small House at Allington.*

The scene depicted occurs on page 67, where the earl comes across Johnny Eames who has fallen asleep on his land in the old Manor woods:

'"Young man," said the voice, "if you want to catch rheumatism, that's the way to do it. Why, it's young Eames, isn't it?"

"Yes, my lord," said Johnny, raising himself up so that he was now sitting, instead of lying, as he looked up into the earl's rosy face.'

Initial letters to the chapter openings facing xvi and xvii.

(xvii) 'There is Mr. Harding coming out of the Deanery', February 1863, facing page 214 with an initial letter design on page 214. To Anthony Trollope, *The Small House at Allington.*

The scene depicted occurs on page 217 where Adolphus Crosbie, outside the Cathedral at Barchester, questions the verger as to the identity of Mr Harding, the precentor:

'"No, Mr. Harding; he that chanted the Litany just now. There he is, sir, coming out of the deanery."

They were now standing at the door leading out from one of the transepts, and Mr. Harding passed them as they were speaking together. He was a little, withered, shambling old man, with bent shoulders, dressed in knee-breeches and long black gaiters, which hung rather loosely about his poor old legs, – rubbing his hands one over the other as he went.'

(xviii) 'And have I not really loved you?', March 1863, facing page 349 with an initial letter design on page 349. To Anthony Trollope, *The Small House at Allington*.

The scene depicted occurs on page 369, when Johnny Eames declares his love for Lily Dale having heard that she is now engaged to his rival, Adolphus Crosbie:

'"And have I not really loved you? Well, never mind. I have said what I came to say, and I will now go. If it ever happens that we are down in the country together, perhaps I may see you again; but never in London. Good-by, Lily." And he put out his hand to her.'

Initial letters to the chapter openings facing xviii and xix.

(xix) 'Mr. Palliser and Lady Dumbello', April 1863, facing page 469 with an initial letter design on page 469. To Anthony Trollope, *The Small House at Allington*.

The scene depicted occurs on page 486, where Lady Dumbello and the young politician and heir of the Duke of Omnium, Plantaganet Palliser, find themselves together:

'He had been in the room nearly an hour when he did at last find himself standing close to Lady Dumbello; – close to her, and without any other very near neighbour.'

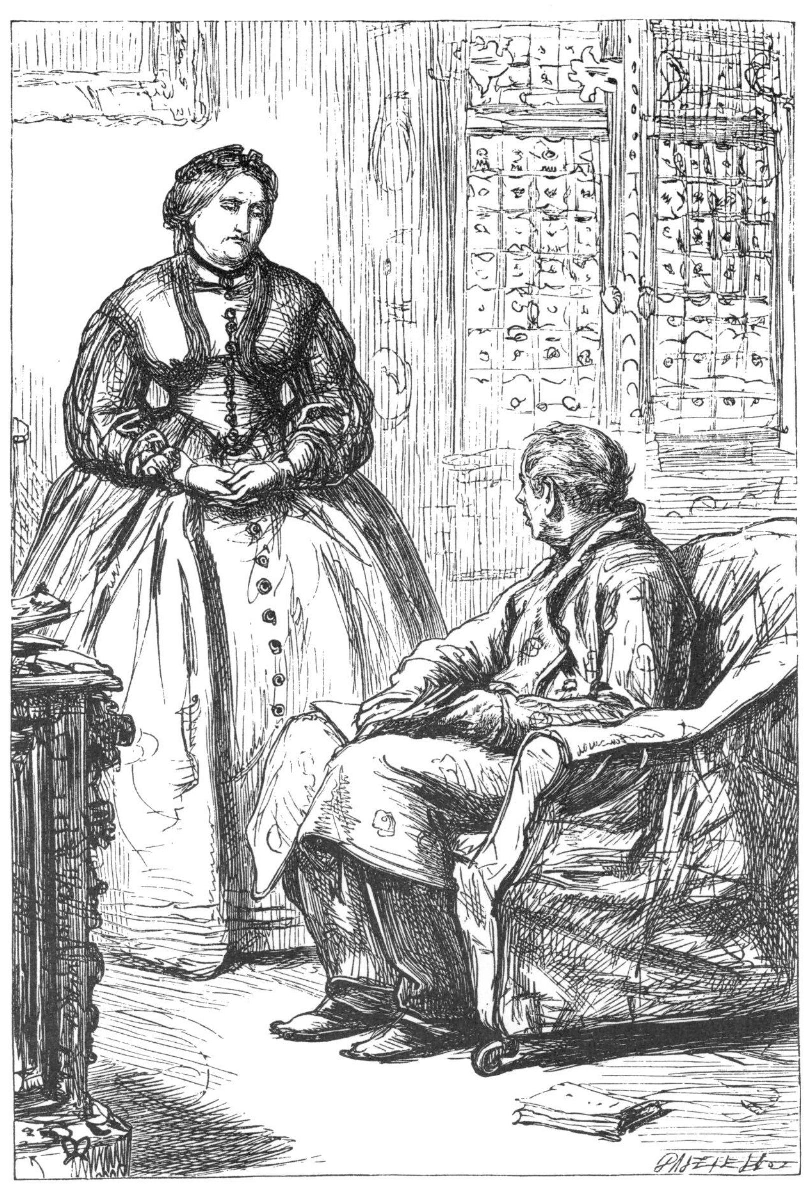

(xx) 'Devotedly attached to the young man!', May 1863, facing page 657 with an initial letter design on page 657. To Anthony Trollope, *The Small House at Allington*.

The scene depicted occurs on page 672, where the earl speaks scornfully of Crosbie's betrothal to Lady Alexandrina de Courcy having thrown over Lily Dale:

'"I really think she'll be happy, and she is devotedly attached to the young man."
"Devotedly attached to the young man!" The tone and manner in which the earl repeated these words were such as to warrant an opinion that his lordship might have done very well on the stage had his attention been called to that profession.'

Initial letters to the chapter openings facing xx and xxi.

(xxi) 'The Board', June 1863, facing page 756 with an initial letter design on page 756. To Anthony Trollope, *The Small House at Allington.*

The scene depicted occurs on page 760, where Crosbie goes before the promotion board made up of Sir Raffle Buffle, Mr Optimist, Mr Butterwell and Major Fiasco:

'The Board, as he entered the room, was not such a Board as the public may, perhaps, imagine such Boards to be. There was a round table, with a few pens lying about, and a comfortable leathern arm-chair at the side of it, farthest from the door. Sir Raffle Buffle was leaving his late colleagues, and was standing with his back to the fire-place, talking very loudly.'

(xxii) ‘Won’t you take some more wine?’, July 1863, facing page 59 with an initial letter design on page 59. To Anthony Trollope, *The Small House at Allington.*

The scene depicted occurs on page 69 at the meal at Pawkins’. The earl (Lord de Guest), Johnny Eames and Colonel Dale dine together:

‘“Dale,” said he, “won’t you take some more wine?”
“Nothing more,” said the colonel, still looking at the fire, and shaking his head very slowly.’

Initial letters to the chapter openings facing xxii and xxiii.

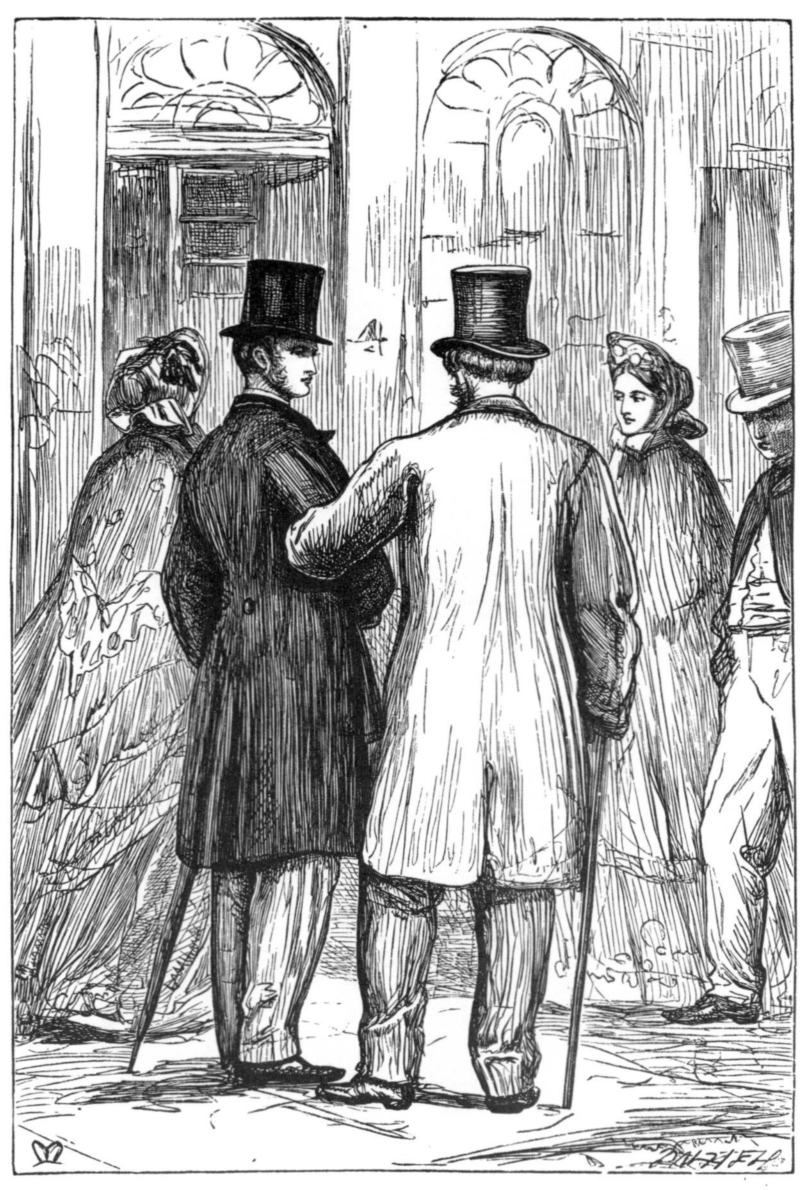

(xxiii) 'And you went in at him on the station?', August 1863, facing page 208 with an initial letter design on page 208. To Anthony Trollope, *The Small House at Allington.*

The scene depicted occurs on page 224, where Cradell speaks with some admiration to Johnny after the latter has fought his rival Crosbie at the station:

'"And you went in at him on the station? asked Cradell, with admiring doubt.
"Yes, I did. If I didn't do it there, where was I to do it? I'd said I would, and therefore when I saw him I did it." Then the whole affair was told as to the black eye, the police, and the superintendent.'

(xxiv) 'Let me beg you to think over the matter again', September 1863, facing page 258 with an initial letter design on page 258. To Anthony Trollope, *The Small House at Allington*.

The scene depicted occurs on page 270, where the squire tries to reason with Mrs Dale to persuade her against leaving the Small House:

'"A quarrel between me and your children would be to me a great calamity, though, perhaps, they might be indifferent to it. But if there were such a quarrel it would afford no reason for their leaving that house. Let me beg you to think over the matter again."'

Initial letters to the chapter openings facing xxiv and xxv.

(xxv) 'That might do', October 1863, facing page 385 with an initial letter design on page 385. To Anthony Trollope, *The Small House at Allington.*

The scene depicted occurs on page 390, where the Ladies Amelia and Alexandrina try to choose a carpet with Adolphus in attendance:

'"That might do," said Alexandrina, gazing upon a magnificent crimson ground through which rivers of yellow meandered, carrying with them in their streams an infinity of blue flowers. And as she spoke she held her head gracefully on one side, and looked down upon the carpet doubtingly.'

(xxvi) '"Mamma," she said at last. "It is all over now, I'm sure."', November 1863, facing page 513 with an initial letter design on page 513. To Anthony Trollope, *The Small House at Allington.*

The scene depicted occurs on page 527 where Lily, who is recovering from scarlatina, speaks with sadness of the marriage of Crosbie to Alexandrina de Courcy:

'"Mamma," she said at last, "it is over now, I'm sure."
"What is over, my dear?"
"He has made that lady his wife. I hope God will bless them, and I pray that they may be happy." As she spoke these words, there was an unwonted solemnity in her tone which startled Mrs. Dale and Bell.'

Initial letters to the chapter openings facing xxvi and xxvii.

(xxvii) 'Why, on earth, on Sunday?', December 1863, facing page 641 with an initial letter design on page 641. To Anthony Trollope, *The Small House at Allington.*

The scene depicted occurs on page 659 where Adolphus Crosbie, now married to Alexandrina, bickers over having to go to her sister in St John's Wood on a Sunday:

'There was, however, one point as to which he could grumble. "Why, on earth, on Sunday?"

"Because Amelia asked me for Sunday. If you are asked for Sunday, you cannot say you'll go on Monday."'

(xxviii) 'Bell, here's the inkstand', January 1864, facing page 1 with an initial letter design on page 1. To Anthony Trollope, *The Small House at Allington*. The scene depicted occurs on page 6, where Lily and Bell are clearing out the house which they are preparing to leave:

'"Oh, Bell, here's the inkstand for which you've been moaning for three years."

"I haven't been moaning for three years; but who could have put it up there?"

"Catch it," said Lily; and she threw the bottle down on to a pile of carpets.'

Initial letters to the chapter openings facing xxviii and xxix.

(xxix) 'She has refused me and it is all over', February 1864, facing page 232 with an initial letter design on page 232. To Anthony Trollope, *The Small House at Allington.*

The scene depicted occurs on page 256. Johnny Eames turns in despair to Lady Julia and tells her that Lily has turned down his proposal of marriage:

'... a gentle step came close up to him, and turning round, he saw that Lady Julia was on the bridge. She was close to him, and had already seen his handiwork. "Has she offended you, John ?" she said.

"Oh, Lady Julia!"

"Has she offended you?"

"She has refused me, and it is all over."

"It may be that she has refused you, and yet it need not be all over. I am sorry you have cut out the name, John. Do you mean to cut it out from your heart?"'

(xxx) Untitled initial letter illustration, April 1864, page 442. To Anthony Trollope, *The Small House at Allington.*

Initial letters to the chapter opening on page 442 and facing xxxi.

(xxxi) 'An Old Song', October 1864, facing page 434 with an initial letter design on page 434. To 'Madame de Monferrato':

'It was at a musical party in the Rue de Rivoli. Marian Campbell, a lovely girl with a lovely voice, whom I had known ever since she was a baby, had just done singing one of Verdi's noisiest bravura airs.'

5. GOOD WORDS [Pp 6214 d]

(i) 'Olaf the Sinner and Olaf the Saint', January 1862, page 25. The story is signed 'H.K.'

'On his bare, brown hand he flung the glowing fire … he let it scorch the skin, and simmer the blood, and bite to the bone.'

(ii) Untitled frontispiece, 1862. To Dinah Mulock (Mrs Craik), *Mistress and Maid*. Reprinted in *Collected Illustrations*, 1866, no.13 (Book Illustrations 38).

The untitled illustration placed as frontispiece refers to the following lines at the end of the novel on page 748 (December 1862). Elizabeth mourns at the grave of her beloved Tom:

'She buried him, herself the only mourner, on a bright summer's day, with the sun shining dazzlingly on the white grave-stones in Kensal Green. The clergyman appeared, read the service, and went away again. A few minutes ended it all. When the undertaker and his men had also departed, she sat down on a bench near, to watch the sexton filling up the grave – Tom's grave.'

(iii) Untitled illustration, January 1862, page 33. To Dinah Mulock (Mrs Craik), *Mistress and Maid*, chapter 1. Reprinted in *Collected Illustrations*, 1866, no.71 (Book Illustrations 38).

'She was a rather tall, awkward, and strongly built girl of about fifteen. This was the first impression the "maid" gave to her "mistresses," the Misses Leaf, when she entered their kitchen, accompanied by her mother, a widow and washerwoman, by name Mrs. Hand. I must confess, when they saw the damsel, the ladies felt a certain twinge of doubt as to whether they had not been rash in offering to take her;'

(iv) Untitled illustration, February 1862, page 97. To Dinah Mulock (Mrs Craik), *Mistress and Maid*, chapter 3. Reprinted in *Collected Illustrations*, 1866, no.58 (Book Illustrations 38). The design was reworked by Millais for the steel-engraved frontispiece to the Hurst and Blackett *Standard Library* edition. See Book Illustrations 17.

The scene depicted actually appears in chapter 4 (page 104):

'"Let me look at them." And Hilary tried to contemplate gravely the scrawled and blotted page, which looked very much as if a large spider had walked into the ink-bottle and then walked out again on a tour of investigation. "What did you want to write?" asked she, suddenly.'

(v) Untitled illustration, March 1862, page 161. To Dinah Mulock (Mrs Craik), *Mistress and Maid*, chapter 5.

The scene depicted is actually in chapter 6 (page 168). Robert Lyon and Hilary are walking together:

'Then casting a glance round, and seeing that Ascott was quite out of ear-shot, he said with that tender fall of the voice that felt, as some poet hath it –

"Like a still embrace," –

"Now, tell me as much as you can about yourself."'

(vi) Untitled illustration, April 1862, page 225. To Dinah Mulock (Mrs Craik), *Mistress and Maid*, chapter 7. Reprinted in *Collected Illustrations*, 1866, no.67 (Book Illustrations 38).

The scene depicted is actually in chapter 9 (page 232):

'And Johanna sat down, with her sweet, calm, long-suffering face turned upwards to that younger one, which was, as youth is apt to be, hot, and worried, and angry. And so they waited till the terminus was almost deserted, and the last cab had driven off, when, suddenly, dashing up the station-yard out of another, came Ascott.'

(vii) Untitled illustration, May 1862, page 289. To Dinah Mulock (Mrs Craik), *Mistress and Maid*, chapter 10. Reprinted in *Collected Illustrations*, 1866, no.64 (Book Illustrations 38).

The scene depicted is actually in chapter 11 (page 295):

'The reading was disturbed by a carriage driving up to the door, and a knock, a tremendously grand and forcible footman's knock, which made Miss Leaf start in her easy-chair.

"But it can't be visitors to us. We know nobody. Sit still, Elizabeth."

It was a visitor, however, though by what ingenuity he found them out, remained, when they came to think of it, a great puzzle. A card was sent in by the dirty servant of Mrs. Jones....'

(viii) Untitled illustration, June 1862, page 353. To Dinah Mulock (Mrs Craik), *Mistress and Maid*, chapter 12. Reprinted in *Collected Illustrations*, 1866, no.39 (Book Illustrations 38).

The scene depicted is in chapter 12 (page 355):

'After trying several pairs – with a fierce, bitter blush at a small hole which the day's walking had worn in her well-darned stockings, and which she was sure the shopman saw, as well as an old lady who sat opposite – Hilary bought the stoutest and plainest of boots.'

(ix) Untitled illustration, July 1862, page 417. To Dinah Mulock (Mrs Craik), *Mistress and Maid*, chapter 14.

The scene depicted is actually in chapter 15 (page 424), as Ascott Leaf is taken by the bailiffs:

'"No; she'll know it quite soon enough. Let her sleep till morning. Elizabeth, look here." He wrote upon a card the address of the place he was to be taken to. "Give Aunt Hilary this. Say, if she can think of a way to get me out of this horrid mess – but I don't deserve it. Never mind. Come on, you fellows."'

(x) Untitled illustration, August 1862, page 481. To Dinah Mulock (Mrs Craik), *Mistress and Maid*, chapter 16. Reprinted in *Collected Illustrations*, 1866, no.69 (Book Illustrations 38).

The scene depicted is in chapter 16 (page 482):

'And with an ingenious movement that just fell short of a push, somehow the woman was got on the other side of the parlour-door, which Elizabeth immediately shut. Then Miss Hilary stretched her hands across the table, and looked up piteously in her servant's face.'

(xi) Untitled illustration, September 1862, page 545. To Dinah Mulock (Mrs Craik), *Mistress and Maid*, chapter 19. Reprinted in *Collected Illustrations*, 1866, no.12 (Book Illustrations 38).

The scene depicted is in chapter 19 (page 546):

'"It is twenty-four hours since he went," she reasoned. "If he had done anything desperate he would have done it at once, and we should have heard of it long before now;"'

(xii) Untitled illustration, October 1862, page 609. To Dinah Mulock (Mrs Craik), *Mistress and Maid*, chapter 21. Reprinted in *Collected Illustrations*, 1866, no.60. (Book Illustrations 38).

The scene depicted occurs at the opening of the chapter:

'It was not a cheerful morning on which to be married. A dense, yellow, London fog, the like of which the Misses Leaf had never yet seen, penetrated into every corner of the parlour at No.15, where they were breakfasting drearily by candle-light, all in their wedding attire.'

(xiii) Untitled illustration, November 1862, page 673. To Dinah Mulock (Mrs Craik), *Mistress and Maid*, chapter 24.

The scene depicted is in chapter 24 (page 677):

'Towards the middle of the night, when her baby was brought to her, and the child instinctively refused its natural food, and began screaming violently, Mrs. Ascott's troubled look returned.'

(xiv) 'Highland Flora', July 1862, page 393. The scene is described on page 392:

'As he was walking down, he heard
A wailing cry o' pain,
An' at the Lochan-side he found
A woman and a wean.'

(xvi) 'O the lark is singing in the sky', January 1864, facing page 64. The poem is signed 'R.B.R.' Reprinted in *Collected Illustrations*, 1866, no.37 (Book Illustrations 38).

'O the lark is singing in the sky,
  A bonny, bonny song;
But there's a bird in my heart, love,
  A-singing all day long.
The soaring lark sinks back to earth –
  His song will soon be o'er;
But the bird in my heart, love,
  Shall sing for evermore.'

(xvii) 'A Scene for a Study', February 1864, facing page 160. Poem by Jean Ingelow (verse 4):

> 'Here is the study the painter wrought;
> A little way off that window glows,
> And the prints of children's feet are brought
> Up to the doorway, athwart the snows,
> And the moonbeam falls like an afterthought,
> And silvers their pathway who now repose.'

(xviii) 'Polly', March 1864, facing page 248. Reprinted in *Collected Illustrations*, 1866, no.30 (Book Illustrations 38).

'Folded hands,
   Saying prayers,
Understands
   Not, nor cares;

Thinks it odd,
   Smiles away;
Yet may God
   Hear her pray!'

(xix) 'The Bridal of Dandelot', April 1864, facing page 304. Reprinted in *Collected Illustrations*, 1866, no.55 (Book Illustrations 38). Poem by Dora Greenwell:

'The word she spake so soft and low
A bird hath ta'en to Dandelot;
He hath not sent her ring or glove,
Or pledge of faith, or gage of love;
He hath not sued for tress of hair,
Or picture next his heart to wear.'

(xx) 'Prince Philibert', June 1864, facing page 481 or page 479 in some copies. Reprinted in *Collected Illustrations*, 1866, no.17 (Book Illustrations 38).

'I went to the pond with him,
(Just like the sea,)
To swim his three-decker,
That's named after me;
His cheeks were like roses;
He knew all the rocks;
He looks like a sailor
In grey knickerbocks.'

(xxi) 'Macleod of Dare', September 1878, facing page 651. Text by William Black:

'This was a strange conversation for two engaged lovers.... Now her eyes never met his. She was afraid.'

(xxii) 'Kept in the Dark', probably to accompany April 1882, frontispiece or facing page 365. See also Book Illustrations 62. Text by Anthony Trollope.

The scene depicted occurs on page 93. The moment is when Cecilia Holt writes to Mr Western to explain her guilt at having been previously engaged to Sir Francis Geraldine. Mr Western is her new lover; she is tortured as to whether to tell him or not, even though nothing improper had ever occurred:

'When the letter was completed, she found it to be one which she could not send.'

6. THE ILLUSTRATED LONDON NEWS [Pp 7611]

(i) 'Christmas Story-Telling', 20 December 1862. Presented separately in the magazine (no page). Engraved by Dalziel. Reduced from 239 × 347 mm (9⅜ × 13⅝ in). Accompanies no text.

8. LONDON SOCIETY [Pp 6004 gp]

(i) 'Ah Me! She was a winsome maid', August 1862, facing page 181. To 'The Border Witch', a poem subtitled 'An Auld-Warld Story' and signed 'TW'.

> 'Ah me! she was a winsome maid,
> Ye couldna fand her marrow
> Had ye sought through a' Scotland braid,
> Frae John o'Groats to Yarrow.'

(ii) '"Yes, Lewis," she said; "Quite satisfied"', Christmas number 1862, facing page 65. To 'The Christmas Wreaths of Rockton':

'And then Margaret turned away with a vague sensation of having lost something; a new consciousness of the strength with which she had suffered herself to cling to the idea of Lilian's companionship; a strange foreboding of a time when she was to be be utterly alone;'

(iii) 'Knightly Worth', September 1864, facing page 193. To 'The Tale of a Chivalrous Life': usually placed as a frontispiece to the 1864 bound volume but in some copies placed opposite the story facing page 247.

The Good Knight accepts the Lady's bounty but insists that the ducats be divided between her two daughters as a marriage portion.

9. ONCE A WEEK [Pp 6004 gi]

(i) 'Magenta', 2 July 1859, page 10. Poem by Tom Taylor:

'Hide, mourner, hide the tears which might such triumphs blur!'

(ii) 'The Grandmother's Apology', 16 July 1859, page 41. Poem by Tennyson.

'I cannot weep for Willy, nor can I weep for the rest;
Only at your age, Annie, I could have wept with the best.'

(iii) 'On the Water', 23 July 1859, page 70. . Poem signed 'Memor'.

'On the water, on the water,
While the summer days were fair,
Whispering words in softest accents
Thro' a veil of drooping hair;'

(iv) 'La Fille Bien gardée', 8 October 1859, page 306. Poem signed 'SB'.

'You'll call me such a worry, Edith, but it is not fun
To be stuck in Temple chambers when October has begun;'

v) 'The Plague of Elliant', 15 October 1859, page 316. Poem translated from the Breton by Tom Taylor.

'Nine children of one house there were
Whom one dead-cart to the grave did bear:
Their mother 'twixt the shafts did fare.'

vi) 'Maude Clare', 5 November 1859, page 382. Poem by Christina Rossetti.

'Take my share of a fickle heart,
Mine of a paltry love:
Take it, or leave it, as you will,
I wash my hands thereof.'

(vii) ‘A Lost Love’, 3 December 1859, page 482. Poem signed ‘R. A. B.’

‘So fair, and yet so desolate;
So wan, and yet so young;
Oh, there is grief too deep for tears,
Too seal’d for tell-tale tongue!
With a faded floweret in her hand,
Poor little hand, so white!
And dim blue eye, from her casement high
She looks upon the night.’

(viii) ‘St. Bartholomew’, 17 December 1859, page 514. Poem signed ‘H. E. E. M.’

‘For to-night is the Lord’s, and his vengeance
Shall redden the waters of Seine;
Let the reapers go forth to the harvest,
And gather this Huguenot grain.’

(ix) ‘The Crown of Love’, 31 December 1859, page 10. Poem by George Meredith.

‘“O death-white mouth! O cast me down!
Thou diest? Then with thee I die.”
“See’st thou the angels with a Crown?
We twain have reach’d the sky.”’

9. Once a Week

SWAIN.Sc

SWAIN.Sc

(x) 'A Wife', 7 January 1860, page 32. Poem signed 'A.':

> 'Face in both hands, she knelt on the carpet;
> The black cloud loosen'd, the storm-rain fell:
> Oh! life has so much to wilder and warp it, –
> One poor heart's day what poet could tell?'

(xi) 'The Head of Bran', 4 February 1860, page 132. Reprinted in *Collected Illustrations*, 1866, no.16 (Book Illustrations 38). Poem by George Meredith:

> 'Princes seven, enchaining hands,
> Bear the live head homeward.
> Lo! it speaks, and still commands;
> Gazing far out foamward.'

(xii) 'Practising', 10 March 1860, page 242. Poem by Shirley Brooks:

> '"Practising, practising." Well, if you're doing it,
> Why do you snub me with answer so tart?
> Since to a friend superficially viewing it
> Practice appears, Jane, a wonderful art.'

(xiii) 'Musa', 16 June 1860, page 598. Poem signed 'E.M.B.':

'Away with you, baby, away to the garden,
And leave ugly Latin to Algernon, do:
He *must* learn the lesson, although it's a hard one,
But, darling, there's plenty of time before you.'

(xiv) 'Master Olaf', 14 July 1860, page 63. From the German, the poem is signed 'L.B.':

'Master Olaf taketh the shoe in hand,
It is too small, but it spread and spread:
And as it grew to the edge of the hoof,
There seizèd the master fear and dread.'

(xv) 'Violet', 28 July 1860, page 140. Poem by Arthur J. Munby:

'She stood where I had used to wait
For her, beneath the gaunt old yew,
And near a column of the gate
That open'd on the avenue.'

(xvi) 'Dark Gordon's Bride', 25 August 1860, page 238. Reprinted in *Collected Illustrations*, 1866, no.27 (Book Illustrations 38). Poem by B. S. Montgomery:

> 'Young Helen has heard the fatal order,
> Her English lover must banish'd be,
> For Gordon, Chief on the Scottish Border,
> Comes hither to bend the wooer's knee.'

(xvii) 'The Meeting', 1 September 1860, page 276. Reprinted in *Collected Illustrations*, 1866, no.59 (Book Illustrations 38). Poem signed 'G. M.':

> 'The girl for her babe made prayerful speech;
> The youth for his love did pray;
> Each cast a wistful look on each,
> And either went their way.'

(xviii) 'The Iceberg', 6 October 1860, page 407. Text by A. Stewart Harrison. See also Book Illustrations 65.

A sailor, Ben, who is attached to Esther, returns from a voyage to discover that she has borne a child by another man. He finds her sewing by the fire and she falls into a faint when she sees him.

9. Once a Week

(xix) 'The Iceberg', 13 October 1860, page 435. Text by A. Stewart Harrison. See also Book Illustrations 65.

Esther dies, but as she does so she declares that she is going to join her former lover.

(xx) 'A Head of Hair for Sale', 3 November 1860, page 519. Unsigned story. A young French woman sells her hair for a pittance.

(xxi) 'Iphis and Anaxarete', 19 January 1861, page 98. Poem by Mary C. F. Münster. A dead woman is discovered by guests coming to celebrate her wedding:

> 'They found what *had been* Iphis, and *was* now
> A ghastly thing to pale the brightest cheek,'

SWAIN Sc

(xxii) 'Thorr's hunt for his Hammer', 26 January 1861, page 126. Poem signed 'G. W. D.':

> *'Thrym quoth:*
> "How is't with Asa-kin?
> How is't with elves?
> Why art thou come alone
> Down into Ogreland?"'

(xxiii) 'Tannhaüser', 17 August 1861, page 211. The translated poem is signed 'L. D. G.':

> 'Your cherry lips avail me nought:
> I loathe them from my heart!
> In the name of all women's honour, I pray
> You'll give me leave to part.'

(xxiv) 'Swing Song', 12 October 1861, page 434. Unsigned poem:

> 'To and fro
> Swang the swing,
> To and fro.'

(xxv) 'Schwerting of Saxony', 4 January 1862, page 43. Poem signed 'A. D.':

'He spoke, the wild flames seized him, – One loud and fearful yell, –
And down on that devoted band the crumbling mansion fell.'

(xxvi) 'The Battle of the Thirty', 1 February 1862, page 155. An unsigned translation of a Breton ballad. Reprinted in *Collected Illustrations*, 1866, no.45 (Book Illustrations 38). This illustrates the second section, 'The Prayer of the Thirty to St. Kado.':

'"Blessèd St. Kado, that guard'st our land,
Strengthen us now in heart and hand;
Grant that to-day, by aid from thee,
Brittany's foes may conquered be."'

(xxvii) 'The Fair Jacobite', 22 February 1862, page 239. This is an independent design, apparently not illustrating any particular text. Reprinted in *Collected Illustrations*, 1866, no.35 (Book Illustrations 38).

(xxviii) Untitled illustration, 15 March 1862, page 309. To Harriet Martineau, *Sister Anna's Probation*. Reprinted in *Collected Illustrations*, 1866, no.25 (Book Illustrations 38), where entitled 'Let us speak together before we sleep'.

The scene depicted occurs on page 314 as Anna, considering becoming a nun, confides in her mother:

'No: I shall not weep for walks on the seashore, nor for birdnesting in the wood, nor for the garden here, nor even this dear room where Eleanor and I have been such friends. But, mother, we are talking presumptuously. Perhaps I may not be judged worthy a year hence.'

(xxix) Untitled illustration, 22 March 1862, page 337. To Harriet Martineau, *Sister Anna's Probation.*

The scene depicted occurs on page 339, where Anna is undergoing her year of probation in the convent:

'One day the three young maidens were sitting at their table of study, silently bending over their work, which was illuminating each a page of a manuscript which was to be printed as a book.... The sister who instructed them criticised their work in the fewest words, leaving them in the intervals.'

(xxx) Untitled illustration, 29 March 1862, page 365. To Harriet Martineau, *Sister Anna's Probation*. Reprinted in *Collected Illustrations*, 1866, no.44 (Book Illustrations 38), where entitled 'Anna and her lover'.

The scene depicted occurs on page 372 where Anna meets her secret lover, Henry Fletcher:

'Her lover he now was, avowedly. He was as careful of her as a spiritual father could be, and as tender as a real father; as reverential as a stranger could be, and as sympathising as a brother: yet he was her lover.'

(xxxi) Untitled illustration, 5 April 1862, page 393. To Harriet Martineau, *Sister Anna's Probation*. Reprinted in *Collected Illustrations*, 1866, no.52 (Book Illustrations 38), where entitled 'Anna rested on her hoe and listened'.

The scene depicted occurs on page 395 in the convent garden:

'Anna was gardening, one morning in March, with Sister Perpetua standing by, talking of the mezereon and the early tulips, and the violets which would soon be fit for perfume-bags, when they heard some shouts from the village. Anna rested on her hoe and listened. Sister Perpetua remarked on the difference between the roar of human voices and that of the sea, to which it is often compared.'

(xxxii) Untitled illustration, 12 April 1862, page 421. To Harriet Martineau, *Sister Anna's Probation.*

The scene depicted occurs at the conclusion of the story on page 426, as Henry and Anna are united:

'... and they were soon hidden in the wood, their horses tied to trees.... The volume was there – untouched since Anna had read in it last. She showed what her last lesson had been: and then they took out their precious book, hiding away its four-legged case. They lived to have a handsome family Bible, in a place of honour in their own hall: but to the end of their days this was the Bible from which they read together.'

(xxxiii) 'Sir Tristem', 22 March 1862, page 350. Poem by William Buchanan:

'Sir Tristem slumbered quietly!
But on his forehead there was light,
And in a trance he seemed to see
The ghostly shores on left and right;'

(xxxiv) 'The Crusader's Wife', 10 May 1862, page 546. Poem translated from the Breton by Tom Taylor.

'For the space of seven long years she wept, a mournful thing,
At the end of seven long years she set herself to sing,'

(xxxv) 'The Chase of the Siren', 31 May 1862, page 630. Poem by Walter Thornbury:

> 'For the madmen run but faster –
> Evil led and evil seeking –
> Caring not for wife or maiden,
> Caring not for child or master.
> All their hope is on the Siren,
> Could they struggle on but faster.'

The final line of the poem reads:

> 'For she hates man – does the Siren.'

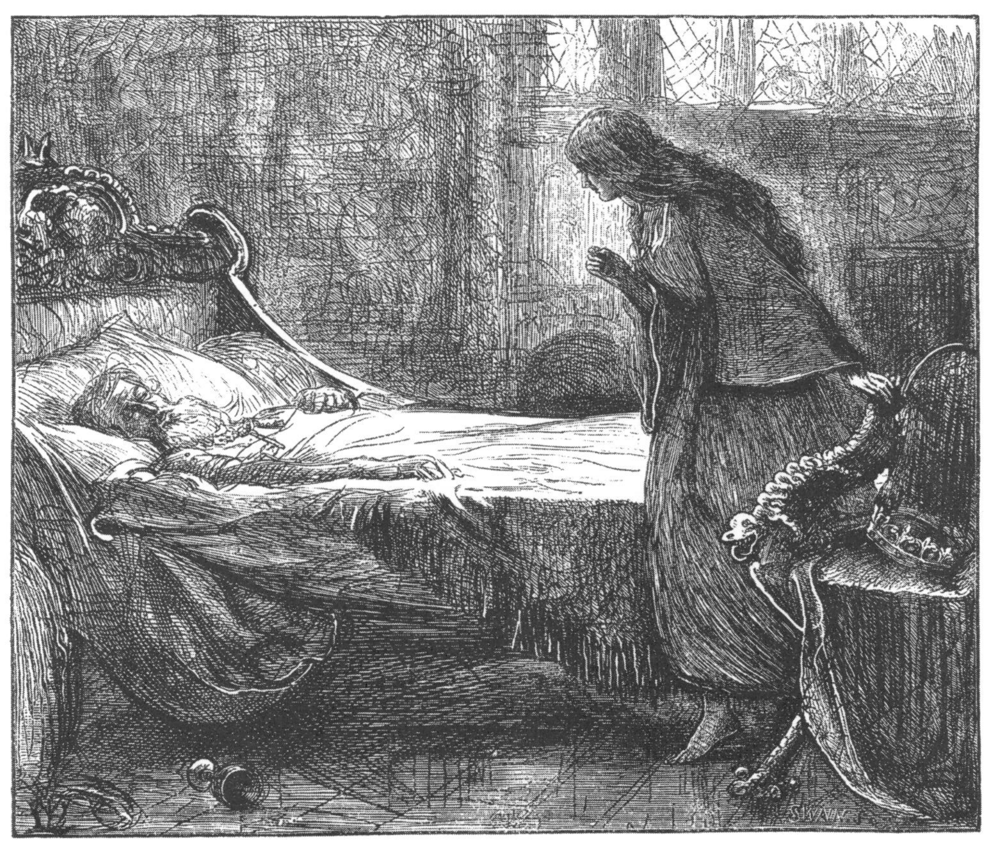

(xxxvi) 'The Drowning of Kaer-Is', 14 June 1862, page 687. Poem translated from the Breton by Tom Taylor. Reprinted in Taylor's *Ballads and Songs of Brittany*, 1865 (see Book Illustrations 30). Also reprinted in *Collected Illustrations*, 1866, no.34 (Book Illustrations 38) where entitled 'I will win the key from my father's side'.

'Whoso had watch'd that night, I weet,
Had seen a maiden stilly fleet
In at the door, on naked feet,

To the old king's side, she hath stolen free,'

(xxxvii) 'Margaret Wilson', 5 July 1862, page 42. Reprinted in *Collected Illustrations*, 1866, no.3 (Book Illustrations 38), where entitled 'Margaret Wilson, the Scottish Martyr'.

The text is taken from her epitaph from Wodrow in the churchyard of Wigton; she was a martyr who died from drowning having been tied to a stake in the sea:

'Murdered for owning Christ supreme
Head of his Church, and no more crime
But her not owning Prelacy,
And not abjuring Presbytery;
Within the sea, tied to a stake,
She suffered for Christ Jesu's sake.'

(xxxviii) Untitled illustration, 19 July 1862, page 85. To Harriet Martineau, *The Anglers of the Dove*. The tale (called 'An Historiette') is based on Bess of Hardwick; the Dove referred to in the title is the River Dove. Reprinted in *Collected Illustrations*, 1866, no.74 (Book Illustrations 38), where entitled 'Farmer Chell's Kitchen'.

The scene depicted occurs on page 89. Polly Chell is about to return home:

'Polly was wanted at home, – sorely wanted. Her father was in from the field; her mother was weary with the tending of the ewes, and had brought in two or three half alive lambs, which began to make a noise as the warmth of the chimney corner revived them. The good wife remarked that they had made her neglect her own dear lamb; and she leaned over the crib in which lay her sick child, quietly crying because the noise prevented him from sleeping.'

(xxxix) Untitled illustration, 26 July 1862, page 113. To Harriet Martineau, *The Anglers of the Dove*. Reprinted in *Collected Illustrations*, 1866, no.51 (Book Illustrations 38), where entitled 'Sorting the prey'.

The scene depicted occurs on page 114 as Stansbury and Felton sort their catch:

'The party sat down to sort the prey. The finest were taken charge of by Sampson, who marched off with the pannier on his shoulder. The gentlemen amused themselves with stringing the rest on birch twigs and long rushes.'

(xl) Untitled illustration, 2 August 1862 , page 141. To Harriet Martineau, *The Anglers of the Dove*. Reprinted in *Collected Illustrations*, 1866, no.14 (Book Illustrations 38), where entitled 'Mary Queen of Scots at Buxton'.

The scene depicted occurs on page 143 where Bess's husband, despite being ill, is able to catch a glimpse of Mary, Queen of Scots:

'And she so arranged a mirror, fixed outside the window, as that the Earl could command a portion of one of the garden walks, on which Mary of Scotland presently appeared, pacing slowly, and followed by two of her ladies. The Earl observed that she looked not otherwise than in health, but very thoughtful.'

(xli) Untitled illustration, 9 August 1862, page 169. To Harriet Martineau, *The Anglers of the Dove.*

The scene depicted occurs on page 169. Polly sits in reverie following the death of her young brother:

'She was full of awe. She had seen more than one person die; but she had never before been alone with death. The hour was too solemn for tears.'

(xlii) Untitled illustration, 16 August 1862, page 197. To Harriet Martineau, *The Anglers of the Dove.*

The scene depicted occurs on page 200. It is apparently the day of Mary, Queen of Scots' accession to the throne, but in truth she is shortly to be arrested:

'Polly, who had been gazing abroad through Father Berthon's glass, now announced that there were bonfires on all the hills round, and cressets were already alight on every church steeple. The whole country would be aglow, as soon as it was dark.'

(xliii) 'Maid Avoraine', 19 July 1862, page 98. Poem by R. Williams Buchanan:

'When at the cottage door they stopt,
Down at his feet the maiden dropt,
Worn with the weary race;
But Gawain leapt to earth in bliss,
And caught her to him with a kiss ...'

(xliv) 'The Mite of Dorcas', 16 August 1862, page 224. This does not appear to relate to any text in the magazine. Reprinted in *Collected Illustrations*, 1866, no 41 (Book Illustrations 38).

(xlv) 'The Spirit of the Vanished Island', 8 November 1862, page 546. Poem by Mrs Acton Tindal:

> 'But when the morning lights the sky,
> Men see that Indian gliding by,
> With airy plume and misty vest,
> An infant shadow on her breast,'

(xlvi) 'The Parting of Ulysses', 6 December 1862, page 658. The text is from Pope's edition of the *Odyssey*:

> 'Rise, rise, my mates! 'tis Circe gives command:
> Our journey calls us; haste, and quit the land.'

SWAIN. Sc

SWAIN.SC

(xlvii) 'Limerick Bells', 20 December 1862, page 710. Poem by Horace Moule. Reprinted in *Collected Illustrations*, 1866, no.66 (Book Illustrations 38), where entitled 'The Monk':

> 'He stood like one forlorn and weary grown,
>   Who listens alway, but who never hears;
> And yet he weeps not, lest the precious tone
>   Be quench'd in drowning tears.'

(xlviii) 'Endymion on Latmos', 3 January 1863, page 42. Poem signed 'R. N. S.':

> 'Rested the silvery moonbeam and streamed on his marvellous beauty,
> Streamed on his golden hair and forehead's roseate marble,
> Chilled to the heart by her kiss, Endymion slumbers on Latmos,
> Never again to awake, ah, me! to the glory of living.'

(xlix) Untitled illustration, 14 February 1863, page 211. To Harriet Martineau, *The Hampdens.* Termed an 'Historiette', the novel is about John Hampden and his refusal to submit to the paying of Ship Money.

The scene depicted occurs at the very opening of the story on page 211:

'"Now you have seen the sea!" said Richard Knightley to his young bride, as they stood looking abroad from a point of the Cornish coast, at sunset, one bright April evening of 1635. "Now you have seen the sea at last!"'

(l) Untitled illustration, 21 February 1863, page 239. To Harriet Martineau, *The Hampdens.* Reprinted in *Collected Illustrations*, 1866, no.31 (Book Illustrations 38), where entitled 'Lady Carew and Margaret'.

Page 242, Lady Carewe and her niece Henrietta:

'Lady Carewe was in no haste to reach the cottages. They were not her only object. She led the way through the flower-garden, and gathered the violets, and lingered over the hyacinths while they were sparkling with dew.'

(li) Untitled illustration, 28 February 1863, page 267. To Harriet Martineau, *The Hampdens.* Reprinted in *Collected Illustrations*, 1866, no.5 (Book Illustrations 38), where entitled 'A Scene in Merrie England'.

Page 270, the Hampdens approaching their home:

'As the party approached the mansion, several horses in the paddock came rushing to the fence to see the arrival of their bretheren in the cavalcade.... There were guests.'

SWAIN.

(lii) Untitled illustration, 7 March 1863, page 281. To Harriet Martineau, *The Hampdens.*

Page 285, Sir Oliver suggests the King might be entertained at Biggin House:

'The girls looked at each other in some dismay at the thought of having to play hostess to such a party.
"I agree with you", said Sir Oliver, looking round upon the somewhat dingy walls and shabby furniture of the great dining- room in which they sat.'

(liii) Untitled illustration, 14 March 1863, page 309. To Harriet Martineau, *The Hampdens.*

Perhaps page 313, in which Henrietta ponders in her room about the journey her uncle wants her to undertake the following day:

'Henrietta might be excused for wondering, while her hair was brushed that night, whose wits were astray now.'

(liv) Untitled illustration, 21 March 1863, page 337. To Harriet Martineau, *The Hampdens.*

Page 342 where Harry speaks to Henrietta about their love. It is difficult to be certain, however, if this is the exact point in the narrative that is being shown.

'We have both been weak and passionate, – too like idle children for so serious a time and so deep a love. We must help each other, and God will perhaps forgive and strengthen us.'

SWAIN

SWAIN

(lv) Untitled illustration, 28 March 1863, page 365. To Harriet Martineau, *The Hampdens.*

The scene depicted appears to be the one on page 366, and seems to show Henrietta in her room discovering concealed letters:

'... she could only receive letters as they came; and they came in all manner of strange ways. Sometimes she found one in her work-basket or her dressing box;'

(lvi) Untitled illustration, 4 April 1863, page 393. To Harriet Martineau, *The Hampdens.* Reprinted in *Collected Illustrations*, 1866, no.76 (Book Illustrations 38), where entitled 'Doing Royal Errands in Merrie England', which is the chapter title.

Page 394 as Harry and Henrietta ride away from London towards Biggin House:

'As the travellers were passing a field of ripening wheat, Henrietta was nearly thrown by the shying of her horse, and Harry was angry accordingly, till he had found that no mischief was done.'

(lvii) Untitled illustration, 11 April 1863, page 421. To Harriet Martineau, *The Hampdens.*

Page 428, where John Hampden speaks to his daughter after his escape:

'"You see, my daughter," said Mr. Hampden, when he took Harry's seat by Henrietta's couch, "you see what it is to trust persons to whom superstition is more dear than the most indispensable and common virtue. You see what it is to be the messenger and tool of persons to whom power is worth any perfidy."'

SWAIN.Sc

SWAIN Sc

(lviii) Untitled illustration, 18 April 1863, page 449. To Harriet Martineau, *The Hampdens.*

Page 452. Henrietta passes the remainder of her life alone in France:

'... Henrietta was soon in retreat for life in the Queen's nunnery at Chaillot.... She did what she could: she prayed for them [the souls of her father and husband] as long as she lived....'

(lix) 'Hacho, the Dane; or The Bishop's Ransom', 24 October 1863, page 504. Poem signed 'C. H. W.'

'Hark! an answer. No, 'tis Echo
Singing but the same refrain,
"Did the Bishop's promised blessing
Ever bring it back again?"'

(lx) Untitled illustration, 24 October 1863, page 491. To Harriet Martineau, *Son Christopher.* Styled an 'Historiette', the tale involves a Protestant family living in Dorset in 1685 and the Monmouth Rebellion.

The scene depicted here occurs on page 493, where Christopher Battiscombe confides in his father:

'"It is certainly true," Christopher declared, when he was satisfied that he could not be heard beyond the fireside, "it is certainly true that the king died a Catholic."'

(lxi) Untitled illustration, 31 October 1863, page 519. To Harriet Martineau, *Son Christopher.*

The scene depicted occurs on page 522, when constables break into the Battiscombes' house searching for subversive material. Forrest Reid (op. cit. p.80) describes Joanna as a boy.

'Finally, they turned upon poor little Joanna, who was sitting on a low stool, reading her new book [*The Pilgrim's Progress*], with her hands at her ears.'

(lxii) Untitled illustration, 7 November1863, page 547. To Harriet Martineau, *Son Christopher.*

The scene depicted occurs on page 551, where Squire Battiscombe meets Monmouth in Lyme Regis:

'He [Monmouth] threw himself into a large chair, and desired his visitor to take the other, remarking that in these fatiguing days, it was well to repose themselves while they could.

The Squire, however, only bowed without seating himself.'

(lxiii) Untitled illustration, 14 November 1863, page 575. To Harriet Martineau, *Son Christopher.* Reprinted in *Collected Illustrations*, 1866, no.18 (Book Illustrations 38), where entitled 'Watching their idol as he galloped away'.

The scene depicted occurs on page 578. The two sisters watch Christopher as he rides to Taunton to join Monmouth's Rebellion:

'"He is in great spirits," Arabella observed to her sister, as they stood at the farmyard gate, watching their idol as he galloped away over the Down.'

(lxiv) Untitled illustration, 21 November 1863, page 603. To Harriet Martineau, *Son Christopher.*

The scene depicted occurs on page 606. Monmouth sends for Christopher's little sister, Joanna:

'The Duke actually remembered the child again. In the evening he sent a coach for her. She was in bed; but no difficulty was made about dressing and despatching her, duly attended, to the mansion occupied by the Duke and his staff.'

(lxv) Untitled illustration, 28 November 1863, page 631. To Harriet Martineau, *Son Christopher.*

The scene shown here is difficult to identify. It possibly refers to one on page 632, shortly after Monmouth has declared himself king:

'He was proclaimed in Taunton market-place under the title of James the Second: but the people did not like the name, and called him "King Monmouth" still.'

(lxvi) Untitled illustration, 5 December 1863, page 659. To Harriet Martineau, *Son Christopher.*

The scene depicted appears to be one occurring in the following chapter, on page 689. The rebellion has been crushed and Christopher, as a close aide to Monmouth, is under arrest. The Battiscombe family has gathered for a service at home. Lady Alice has been beheaded for sheltering fugitives and supporters of Monmouth. A storm has come up:

'The tempest was not unwelcome to any; and the children were permitted to remain and see it out. Joanna sat on her father's knee; and she did not hide her face from the brightest flash. So had they all striven this day, her father said, not to flinch from the lightnings of terror and woe which God had sent to try their souls.'

(lxvii) Untitled illustration, 12 December 1863, page 687. To Harriet Martineau, *Son Christopher*.

The scene depicted is at the conclusion of the story on page 690. The Battiscombes leave home, forced out by circumstance:

'The Battiscombes soon left the home in which their fathers had dwelt for generations.... The reason for their removing to a small house on the shore was that their property was so much reduced by the imposition of fines and securities, that they must descend to a humbler mode of life. Elizabeth was one with them – as firmly fixed with them for a life of duty and devotion – as wedded to their martyr as a nun could be in her convent as the spouse of Christ.'

(lxviii) 'Death Dealing Arrows', 25 January 1868, page 79. No text.

(lxix) 'Taking his Ease', 25 December 1868 (*Once a Year*), facing page 64.

The illustration shows a rather wooden drawing of a resting boy, in a boater, with a lake in the background. Although this appears to illustrate no text in the magazine, the unattributed lines beneath the design read as follows:

> 'And of the traced the uplands to survey,
> When o'er the sky advanced the kindling dawn,
> The crimson cloud, blue main, and mountain grey,
> And lake, dim-gleaming on the smoky lawn:
> For to the west the long long vale withdrawn
> Where twilight loves to linger for awhile.'

10. PUNCH [Pp 5270]

(i) 'It is the Chapeau Blanc, The White Witness', 21 March 1863, page 115. Reduced from 112 × 168 mm (4⅜ × 6⅝ in).

9. Once a Week 10. Punch

11. PUNCH ALMANACK, 1865 [Pp 5276 1-3]

(i) 'Mr. Vandyke Brown, having left the Dress on the Lay Figure carefully arranged, goes out for his usual exercise, and this is how the Boys took advantage of his absence'. Page un-numbered.

The girls look on as the boys cane the lay figure.

12. SAINT PAULS [Pp6004 gl]

'Phineas Finn the Irish Member', October 1867 to May 1869. 20 illustrations. Text by Anthony Trollope.

(i) 'One kiss before we part', facing page 118.

The scene depicted occurs on page 118. Phineas Finn takes his leave from his childhood sweetheart, Mary Flood Jones:

'"Mary," said he, taking her in his arms, without a single word of love-making beyond what the reader has heard, – "one kiss before we part."
"No, Phineas, no!" But the kiss had been taken and given before she had even answered him.'

(iii) 'I wish you would be in earnest with me', facing page 374 or 375. To Anthony Trollope, *Phineas Finn the Irish Member.*

The scene depicted occurs on page 375 during a discussion between Lady Laura Standish and Violet Effingham:

> '"If you do marry, Violet, you must choose some one man out of the lot."
> "That's quite true, my dear. I certainly can't marry them all."
> "And how do you mean to make the choice?"
> "I don't know. I suppose I shall toss up."
> "I wish you would be in earnest with me."'

(ii) 'You don't quite know Mr. Kennedy yet', facing page 247. To Anthony Trollope, *Phineas Finn the Irish Member.*

The scene depicted occurs on page 247, where Lady Laura Standish speaks to Phineas about Mr Kennedy at Lord Brentford's dinner:

'"Do you expect to hear much of an opinion from Mr. Kennedy?"
"Yes I do.You don't quite know Mr. Kennedy yet. And you must remember that he will say more to me than he will to you."'

(iv) 'I wish to regard you as a dear friend, – both of my own and of my husband', facing page 509. To Anthony Trollope, *Phineas Finn the Irish Member*.

The scene depicted occurs on page 509. Phineas has been pipped at the post for the hand of Lady Laura by the lacklustre Mr Kennedy:

'"I, poor, penniless, plain simple fool that I am, have been ass enough to love you, Lady Laura Standish; and I brought you up here to-day to ask you to share with me – my nothingness. And this I have done on soil that is to be all your own. Tell me that you regard me as a conceited fool, – as a bewildered idiot."

(v) 'Laura, would you mind leaving me and Miss Effingham alone for a few minutes?', facing page 637 or 631 in some copies. To Anthony Trollope, *Phineas Finn the Irish Member.*

The scene depicted occurs on page 637, where Lord Chiltern makes an attempt to persuade Violet Effingham to marry him:

'"Laura, would you mind leaving me and Miss Effingham alone for a few minutes?"

Lady Laura got up, and so also did Miss Effingham. "For what purpose?" said the latter. "It cannot be for any good purpose."

"At any rate I wish it, and I will not harm you."'

(vi) 'And do be punctual, Mr. Finn', facing page 750 or 751. To Anthony Trollope, *Phineas Finn the Irish Member*.

The scene depicted occurs on page 750 between Phineas and Mr Clarkson:

'"Suppose we say Monday, – or Tuesday. Tuesday morning at eleven. And do be punctual Mr. Finn."'

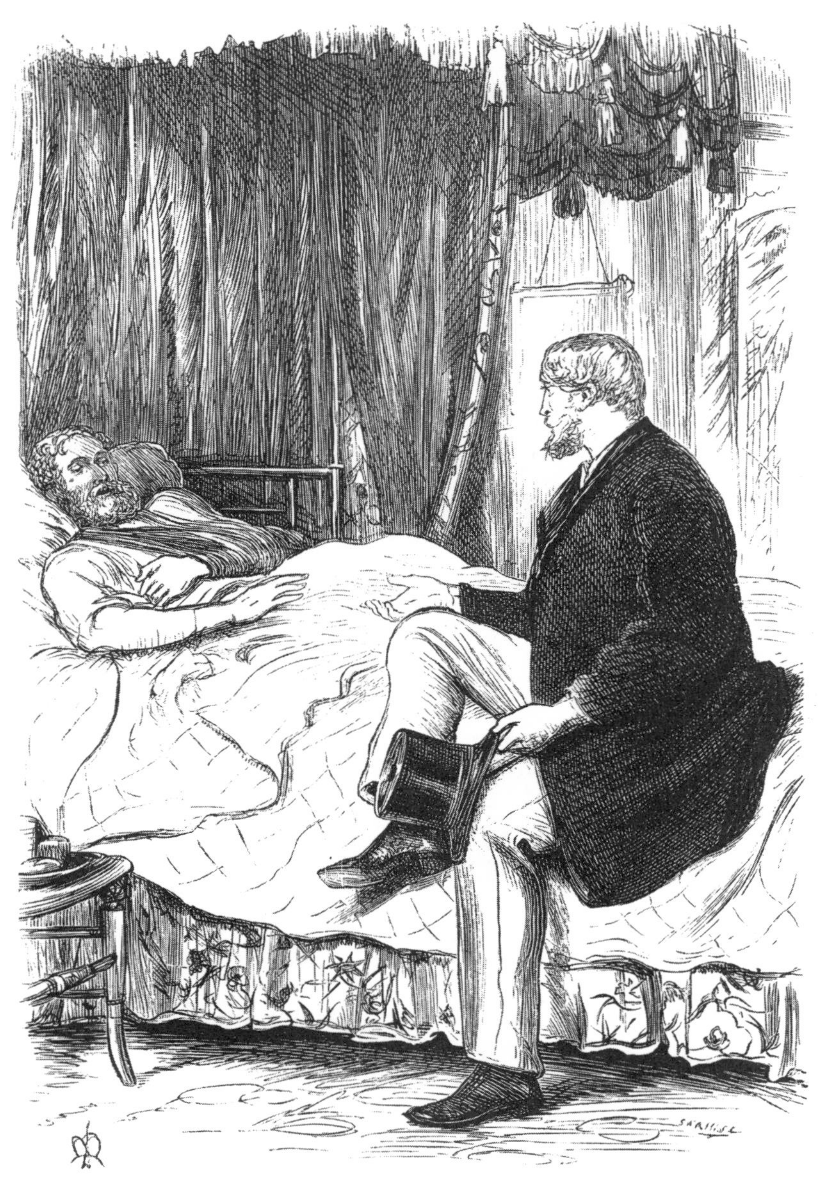

(vii) 'But you Irish fellows always ride', facing page 113. To Anthony Trollope, *Phineas Finn the Irish Member.*

The scene depicted occurs on page 113, where Phineas is at Lord Chiltern's bedside after the latter's fall:

'"That was a good run though, wasn't it?" said Lord Chiltern as Phineas took his leave. "And, by George, Phineas, you rode Bonebreaker so well, that you shall have him as often as you'll come down. I don't know how it is, but you Irish fellows always ride."'

(ix) 'I will send for Dr. Macnuthrie at once', facing page 376 or 377. To Anthony Trollope, *Phineas Finn the Irish Member.*

The scene depicted occurs on page 377, where Lady Laura (now married to Mr Kennedy) realises to her dismay that she does not love her dull husband:

'"Oh dear, oh dear! what am I to do?" Then she threw herself down upon the sofa, and put both her hands up to her temples.

"I will send for Dr. Macnuthrie at once," said Mr. Kennedy walking towards the door very slowly, and speaking as slowly as he walked.'

(viii) ‘May I give him your love?’, facing page 253. To Anthony Trollope, *Phineas Finn the Irish Member.*

The scene depicted occurs on page 253, where Lady Laura and Violet discuss Lord Chiltern’s love for the latter:

‘“I know what I may do, Laura, and I know what I mayn’t; and I won’t be led either by you or by my aunt.”

“May I give him your love?”

“No; – because you’ll give it in a wrong spirit.”’

(x) 'I do not choose that there should be a riot here', facing page 510 or 511. To Anthony Trollope, *Phineas Finn the Irish Member*.

The scene depicted occurs on page 510, where Lord Chiltern and Phineas nearly come to blows over Violet:

'"Then, sir, –" and now Lord Chiltern advanced another step and raised his hand as though he were about to put it with some form of violence on the person of his rival.

"Stop, Chiltern," said Phineas, stepping back, so that there was some article of furniture between him and his adversary. "I do not choose that there should be a riot here."'

(xi) 'You ought to have known. Of course she is in town', facing page 638. To Anthony Trollope, *Phineas Finn the Irish Member.*

The scene depicted occurs on page 638. Phineas meets Violet and Lord Fawn at Mr Palliser's:

'"I did not even know that Lady Baldock was in town."

"You ought to have known. Of course she is in town. Where do you suppose I was living? Lord Fawn was there yesterday, and can tell you that my aunt is quite blooming."'

(xii) 'It's the system as I hates, and not you, Mr. Finn', facing page 747. To Anthony Trollope, *Phineas Finn the Irish Member*.

The scene depicted occurs on pages 746–7. Mr Bunce voices his criticism of government to Phineas:

'"We've got to change a deal yet, Mr. Finn, and we'll do it. When a young man as has liberal feelings gets into Parliament, he shouldn't be snapped up and brought into the governing business just because he's poor and wants a salary. They don't do it that way in the States; and they won't do it that way here long. It's the system as I hates, and not you, Mr. Finn."'

(xiii) 'The fact is, mamma, I love him', facing page 128. To Anthony Trollope, *Phineas Finn the Irish Member.*

The scene depicted occurs on page 128. Mary Flood Jones pours out her heart to her mother and realises that Phineas is not in love with her:

'"The fact is, mamma, I love him. I cannot help it. If he ever chooses to come for me, here I am. If he does not, I will bear it as well as I can. It may be very mean of me, but it's true."'

(xiv) 'So she burned the morsel of paper', facing page 233. To Anthony Trollope, *Phineas Finn the Irish Member.*

The scene depicted occurs on page 233. Laura Kennedy has heard the news of Phineas's election via a telegram from her cousin. However, her husband believes that the telegram has come from Phineas himself:

'Lady Laura resolved that her husband should never see those innocent but rather undignified words. The occasion had become one of importance, and such words were unworthy of it. Besides, she would not condescend to defend herself by bringing forward a telegram as evidence in her favour. So she burned the morsel of paper.'

(xv) 'You must come', facing page 381. To Anthony Trollope, *Phineas Finn the Irish Member.*

The scene depicted occurs on page 381 and is a meeting between the Duke of Omnium and Madame Max Goesler:

'And she put out her finger and touched his arm as she spoke. Her hand was very fair, and her fingers were bright with rich gems. To men such as the Duke, a hand, to be quite fair, should be bright with rich gems. "You must come," she said, – not imploring him now but commanding him.'

(xvi) 'And I ain't in a hurry either, – am I, Mamma?', facing either page 502 or 503. To Anthony Trollope, *Phineas Finn the Irish Member.*

The scene depicted occurs on page 503 between Lady Glencora, her son, and the Duke:

'"He will be a duke quite as soon as he wants to be a duke. He likes the House of Commons better than the strawberry leaves I fancy. There is not a man in England less in a hurry than he is." …

"And I ain't in a hurry either, – am I mamma ?" said the little future Lord Silverbridge.'

(xvii) 'Phineas had no alternative but to read the letter', facing page 636 (incorrectly placed in the British Library copy facing page 626). To Anthony Trollope, *Phineas Finn the Irish Member*.

The scene depicted occurs on page 636. Laura Kennedy has now left her husband and wants Phineas to read the letter she has sent to him:

'"Mr. Kennedy has my letter by this time, and I go from hence home with my father."

"Do you wish that I should read the letter?"

"Yes, – certainly. I wish that you should read it. Should I ever meet him again, I shall tell him that you saw it." …

Phineas had no alternative but to read the letter.'

(xviii) 'I mean what I say. Why should I care?', facing page 738 or 739. To Anthony Trollope, *Phineas Finn the Irish Member*.

The scene depicted occurs on page 739. Mary Flood Jones walks musing with her friend Barbara Finn (Phineas's mother):

'"I am sure, my dear, that he is engaged to nobody," said Barbara Finn.
"And I am sure, my dear," said Mary, "that I do not care whether he is or is not."
"What do you mean, Mary?"
"I mean what I say. Why should I care? Five years ago I had a foolish dream, and now I am awake again."'

(xix) 'Ever your own, with all the love of her heart, MARY F. JONES', facing page 103. To Anthony Trollope, *Phineas Finn the Irish Member.*

The scene depicted occurs on pages 102–3, where Mary writes a lover's letter to Phineas:

'"As long as I can have two or three dear, sweet, loving words, I shall be as happy as a queen....

Ever your own, with all the love of her heart,

MARY F. JONES"'

(xx) 'Oh, Phineas; surely a thousand a year will be very nice.', facing page 256. To Anthony Trollope, *Phineas Finn the Irish Member*.

The scene depicted occurs on page 256, the conclusion of the novel. Phineas has just heard that he has been appointed a poor-law inspector in Cork:

'"Oh, Phineas; surely a thousand a-year will be very nice."
"It will be certain," said Phineas, "and then we can be married to-morrow."
"But I have been making up my mind to wait ever so long," said Mary.
"Then your mind must be unmade," said Phineas.

What was the nature of the reply to Lord Cantrip the reader may imagine, and thus we will leave our hero an Inspector of Poor Houses in the County of Cork.'

INDEX